Be Your Own Miracle

MASTER YOUR MINDSET, FUEL YOUR FAITH AND HEAL THROUGH ADVERSITY

Kathryn Mills

BALBOA.PRESS
A DIVISION OF HAY HOUSE

Balboa Press books may be ordered through booksellers or by contacting:

Balboa Press
A Division of Hay House
1663 Liberty Drive
Bloomington, IN 47403
www.balboapress.com.au
AU TFN: 1 800 844 925 (Toll Free inside Australia)
AU Local: (02) 8310 7086 (+61 2 8310 7086 from outside Australia)

Print information available on the last page.

ISBN: 978-1-9822-9509-7 (sc)
ISBN: 978-1-9822-9510-3 (e)

Balboa Press rev. date: 09/02/2022

Your spiritual guide on healing cancer, stress and overwhelm by activating your inner power, intuition and divine connection

mir·acle

['mɪrək(ə)l]

NOUN

> an extraordinary and welcome event that is not explicable by natural or scientific laws and is therefore attributed to a divine agency:
>
> *"the miracle of rising from the grave*

supernatural phenomenon

Dedication

This book is dedicated to my gorgeous daughter Chanel, my inspiration, my driving force, my motivation, my WHY.

Every single day.

"You have the power to heal your life, and you need to know that.
We think so often that we are helpless, but we're not.
We always have the power of our minds... claim
and consciously use your power."
~ Louise Hay

Contents

Welcome

"We are all damaged. We have all been hurt. We have all had to learn painful lessons. We are all recovering from some mistake, loss, betrayal, abuse, injustice, or misfortune. All of life is a process of recovery that never ends. We each must find ways to accept and move through the pain and to pick ourselves back up. For each pang of grief, depression, doubt, or despair there is an inverse toward renewal coming to you in time. Each tragedy is an announcement that some good will indeed come in time. Be patient with yourself." ~ Bryant McGill

Just as those very words above describe, this book was ultimately brought to life through a mixed bag of big, brutal lessons in the university of life. Trials of virtual destruction, pain, deep betrayals, incredible loss, grief, heartache, heartbreak, to sheer joy, the importance of humour, loyalty, and friendship.

To now.
The present.
The catalyst.

A frightening and fast freefall through the sudden and shocking diagnosis of secondary, incurable, inoperable stage 4 brain cancer, without any proverbial parachute or safety net to catch me.
To then be compelled by an internal force, to step up and fight.
And ultimately sit down and write.

This book is about the power of shifting your perspective and how, even though you may be facing a major life event or challenge in this present moment, that we always, always, always have a choice in how we perceive it and then handle it. You may not be able to control the circumstances but you CAN control how you respond and handle life's tests, trials and adversities.

I have personally infused these pages and words with strength, power and motivation and of course, so much love, to guide, direct and give hope and healing. If you have been rocked by cancer in some way shape or form, or currently experiencing a life-changing personal challenge, major life event, loss or diagnosis, may you find comfort and guidance but also inspiration that today is a brand-new day.

Anything can happen, if you simply open your heart and mind and trust in the unlimited power of the Divine Creator and the universe.

This book is for you, if your world has been torn apart or torn down, you are suddenly dealing with high level stress, deep loss or unfathomable pressure, or you have virtually given up hope or feel completely hopeless. Perhaps there is little internal strength left to fight and you want to give in. Or maybe you are lost, feeling as though you have no direction in life, are stuck in a rut and don't know how to resume or begin again? May this book help guide you to focus your thoughts, balance your emotions and fuel your faith that better days are coming.

Through sharing my journey and stories with you, my wish is that it provides inspiration but also a clear path outward and upwards, along with the message you need to hear, delivered at the right time.
I have always said - I am just the messenger.

There are no coincidences, and nothing is by chance. Life always places what you need in front of you at exactly the right time. You chose this book for a reason. It may be to read one sentence, one paragraph, one chapter, or the entire book! Take what resonates and leave the rest. You will know when you read it. It will land in the core of your being and deep within your SOUL.

My wish is for you to feel the full force of my strength, spirit and energy in every single word and may you find the inspiration, resilience and sheer will to take back your power, move forward and BE YOUR OWN MIRACLE.

••

"The natural healing force within each one of us is the greatest force in getting well." ~ Hippocrates

••

Divine blessings to each and every one of you.
Kathy xx

THE REDIRECTION
– the back story and catalyst for change

How long is a piece of string?

....

"Just like there's always time for pain, there's always time for healing." ~ Jennifer Brown

....

"The scans have come back. They've found 2 brain bleeds, one at the back of the neck and another above your left eye, along with significant swelling. There are also numerous clusters found in multiple parts of the brain. I'm sorry to say, you've got incurable, inoperable stage 4 brain cancer. It has metastasized from somewhere in your body. Looking at the progression and the vast number of lesions in the brain and body, you have maybe 6 months to live. I'm sorry. There's nothing we can do. I suggest you call your family."

BOOM.
You could have knocked me over with a feather.
Completely and utterly shell shocked.

On Friday February 5, 2021, after 10 hours in Emergency, following every conceivable test, feeling like a human science project and with no one around me for solace or support, that was the news and the delivery with which it was given. Blunt. Raw. No softness or tact. I felt as though someone had punched me multiple times in the stomach. I just sat there, virtually frozen with shock and feeling like I couldn't breathe.

As the Ward Doctor left my emergency bay room that evening I burst into tears in sheer disbelief. My entire world shattered into a million pieces in less than 2 minutes.
And life as they say, from that moment on, was never the same again.

This was the catalyst that literally knocked me on my backside and changed my life forever and in so many ways.

As I sat down to write, I thought to myself, *"Where do I even begin?"* My life has been anything but normal. Huge life altering moments scattered throughout; from the time I was a little to the present moment. My mind kept repeating, *"How on earth do I begin this story?"* Some of it may seem extreme for those whose lives have been virtually effortless and blessed. On the flipside, it may seem like the proverbial walk in the park compared to what life has thrown at you. In a nutshell, mine has been a rollercoaster of emotional warfare on my soul since I was a small child.

However, I now reflect on these experiences with a different perspective and understanding, that perhaps these lessons, losses, tests, and challenges were merely highlighting where I needed to HEAL, FORGIVE and GROW, on a personal level as well as through my ancestral and generational lineage and how it was all simply setting me up to not only navigate this speed bump with strength, grace and humility, but also to be a light in someone else's world, to guide them through tough times.

We all have a story. And every story is important. This story is unique, although there will be many reading this book that will relate to what I have experienced in life and have endured. I have deep respect for you if you've faced insurmountable giants and are still here and still standing. Embrace your warrior spirit!

Raised on a farm as a child, experiencing a hideous and hard upbringing with a then volatile father, I had buried my two oldest brothers by the time I was 11 years old, both tragically taken in separate accidents and both uncannily on the 23rd (November and June) 10 years apart, 2 marriages, 2 divorces, one to a man with definitive narcissistic traits and the father of my daughter, years of see-sawing domestic violence in the form of verbal, mental and emotional abuse, deep betrayals, affairs, wrong choices and wrong turns as well as major life stresses thrown in at random points along the way.

That is the exceptionally light, and very, very edited version. I'm sure in the future there will be appropriate opportunities to share more when the timing aligns. Yet in spite of being dealt another hard and incomprehensible blow, and through the grace of God, I have survived 100% of these days thus far, and so have you. And I salute you. I salute your bravery, your resilience, your strength, your grit, your determination and your fighting spirit. High level adversities and spiritual warfare are not for the faint-hearted.

Therefore, it is my divine responsibility and mission to share this story to help others in similar situations, to bring strength, light and hope to those who are currently experiencing a crisis, a trauma, an unexpected medical diagnosis like cancer, or even a deep loss of someone special. My soul purpose is to be of service to humanity by educating, inspiring and motivating others through, and out of, life-defining challenges. No matter what, if it helps, heals or changes just one person, if you are reading this, then my book, my story, has been written just for you.

❧ Spirit always has a way of directing us – and connecting us - to the right people and the right message at the right time.
Fast track to now. The catalyst for change. The redirection.

I have always lived by the old saying "You can talk the talk, but can you walk the walk?"
Anyone can talk the talk. And believe me, I've heard it all.
But not everyone can back it up.
Actions trump words every single time.
Don't tell me who you are or what you can do.

Show me.

In this book I keep things real, raw, and at times completely unfiltered and unedited.

Because isn't that life?

Life isn't clean, perfect, polished and pretty every moment of the day. It can be beyond extraordinary and unbelievably beautiful, yet can swiftly shift into chaotic, soul shattering messy moments, to complete upheaval, tears and tragedy and everything in between.

Sometimes all in one day.

And whilst we can all benefit from previous knowledge and information learned on life's lessons through books, courses and speakers, it is only when we walk through the fires of life in real time that we find our own inner strength to endure these trials and major life events.

Spoiler alert – not one single soul will escape life without one, some or more major incidents of sudden shock, loss or tragedy. No one. It is inevitable.

Everyone will eventually freefall from a great height due to some catastrophic life event. That is the sweetness and sadness of life.

The polarity of the two.

None of us are getting out alive. At least not in this dimension.

We came here to grow. In all the ways. Earth school is the hardest and most challenging place our souls have chosen, and in certain chapters of your life, you will feel the burn.

You will feel the suppressed sadness from perhaps an abusive, fearful or less than perfect childhood.

The darkness of grief after losing loved ones.

You may feel the devastation and disbelief that comes with divorce.

The difficulties and challenges attached to raising children.

The deep pain of betrayal from partners, false friends or colleagues.

The cold, harsh, wintery chapters of lack and scarcity in life.

Those feelings of intense pressure that seem never ending.

The drained, depleted bank accounts after significant financial loss.

The daily grind of a body struggling under pain or illness.

The relentless, unspoken battles raging in the mind.

The deafening silence and loneliness as life separates and isolates you, placing you in a solitary corner for a hot minute.

Throughout your life you will feel at least a few of these things, perhaps more.

The purpose of this book is to utilise and expand on these major life crises to motivate, strengthen and inspire YOU. I have often been referred to as a MOTIVATOR and truth teller, especially when it involves moving people towards improving their health and lifestyles. Throughout this journey I came to the full realisation that my previous experiences were simply a training ground for this very moment.
So here I am.
Showing up not only as a deep promise to myself and my daughter, but for you.
From heartbreak and heartache to healing, healed, and now, healer.
Healing through words, a little tough love, understanding, compassion, empathy, messages of hope and inspiration where you may be feeling nothing but a deep void.

This is my assignment and God-given purpose and gift to the world. Navigating successfully through my own struggles, I have earned my spiritual wings and qualifications to now lift, inspire, influence, support, strengthen, liberate, and help YOU, no matter what you have been through, or are currently going through, no matter where you are in life.

Yes, the stories in this book are mostly about my progression through cancer, however, there is no depth of darkness in what you may be facing right now, or have faced, that the Light cannot touch and transform.

You just have to BELIEVE.

> "…..consider the possibility that even your most painful experiences are gifts in this moment that you are yet to realise and understand… …"

MIRACLE INSPIRATION: Victory begins in the dark.

The power that is going to save you is coming from the inside.
Deep inside of you.
We all have this ability.
It just needs to be turned on.
Throughout this book you are going to either find it or strengthen it.
Or both.

If I can do it, you can too.
It's time to BE YOUR OWN MIRACLE.

••

"A lot of people say they want to get out of pain, and I'm sure that's true, but they aren't willing to make healing a high priority. They aren't willing to look inside to see the source of their pain in order to deal with it." ~ Lindsay Wagner

••

THE JOURNEY BEGINS –
overcoming overwhelm, the shell shock, what to do and how to cope after picking yourself up off the floor

....

> "One must still have chaos in oneself to be able to give birth to a dancing star." ~ Friedrich Nietzsche

....

People often ask me whether I had any signs or symptoms in the lead up to this day. In all honesty, no. Not really. As I think back, there was nothing definitive until the weekend prior. I took my daughter down to the pool as it was a hot January day for a play and a swim. As I lay on the sunlounge, I remember feeling tired, a slight headache and unusually off balance. I was never one to experience headaches and so simply brushed it off as having had a big week, juggling too many things, and probably not enough water.

It wasn't until I took my first step into the pool that I felt uneasy and even more unsteady. As I tentatively placed my foot down, I remember my leg feeling as though it was made of concrete, quite heavy, misjudging the height of the pavers to the step and landing on it with a thud. I thought to myself, *"what is going on here? That's not normal."* I continued to cautiously place my feet down onto the last two steps and into the water. The pressure in my head had now intensified and my entire body just felt off.

Internally I was slightly concerned and wondered what on earth was happening. I glanced up to see Chanel at the other end of the pool with some of the building's residents, enjoying the sunshine and the beautiful day. As I swam over to the other side of the pool to the safety of the ladder, my body felt very uncooperative and heavy. I simply could not get there fast enough to latch onto the bar.

After steadying myself for what seemed like only seconds, I looked up at Chanel one more time, before my head dropped backwards and into the water. I had no control over my body.
And I mean none.
Nada.
Zero.

I must have blacked out for maybe 20 seconds, but in that moment in time, it seemed like an eternity. Everything went dark as the water began to rise over my ears. I felt as though I was in a semi-conscious state as my head began to submerge. In that unnerving and somewhat frightening moment I thought I would drown. Instead, and through divine intervention the water snapped me fully awake. The doctors would later explain it was most likely one of the brain bleeds at the back of the neck from the increased swelling and intense pressure in the brain.

I immediately locked my vision onto Chanel and saw her little face just staring at me. She was almost frozen. I called out to her with a few tears of shock in my eyes as she swam down to meet me. I could see the scared look on her little face and reassured her with, *"Mummy is ok sweetheart. I'm ok."* Her response had me holding back a flood of immediate tears as she quietly said, *"Mummy I thought you were going to die."*
In all honesty, for a split second I thought so too.

In my mind as she said this, I intuitively knew I would have been ok as Spirit had placed other people in and around the pool that day. No matter what, if anything more serious would have happened, someone would've come to my immediate rescue.

I hugged her tightly and said, *"Mummy doesn't feel well sweetheart."* I swam very cautiously back to the other side of the pool and steadied myself as I climbed back up onto the steps and out of the water. I laid down again on the sun lounge for about 20-30 minutes to recentre myself and comfort Chanel. My head was pounding at this point and to be honest, I was struggling to internally calm myself down too. Chanel was very clingy, and I could sense her uneasiness and confusion with what she had just witnessed.

When we finally managed to make it back upstairs to the safety of our unit, my head continued to feel very heavy, similar to carrying the weight of a bowling ball and very much out of alignment.

I logically thought, *"Maybe I am coming down with something?"*
So I took it easy for the remainder of the day. That night I slept well and woke up on Monday almost back to normal. I shook it off, thinking it had been a 24-hour virus. School drop offs and pickups continued, as did the gym, work appointments and home routines.

However, this particular week, I had 3 days of consecutive work travelling to the outskirts of Brisbane. Driving every day up and back on a major highway at speed, standing and working all day with other crew and just feeling less than average. On the last day I felt extremely fatigued and washed out.

Walking onto the stand that morning, for the first time in nearly 16 years, I mentioned to my colleagues that I just felt "off", and if they caught me resting in between customer enquiries, to just know I was ok but not feeling my usual happy self. The day would be long and hard however I persevered to the end.

As I left for the long drive home, I made a conscious effort to fill in the time by returning some calls to other work crew and friends. It would be on the very last call that circumstances began to scare me once again. Given it was the middle of summer and the temperatures were high, I placed a bottle of water between my knees to sip on while driving, therefore allowing me to stay alert in peak hour traffic.

Whilst talking to a close girlfriend, I proceeded to grab the bottle, however my hand completely missed it. I tried again. My hand once again swung past the bottle and over to the driver's side door. At this point my internal alarm bells were ringing loudly and my mind was screaming, "*What the hell is going on!?*" On the third attempt I physically looked down and forced my hand to grip the water bottle. This would happen two more times before arriving home. I said a little prayer out loud to God, my guides, and angels as I drove, to please take me home safely, and as I pulled into the basement, I felt a huge surge of relief that I had made it.

My daughter was with her father, so it was just myself at home that night. I felt relieved to be finished for the week, home in my safe place and a quiet peaceful evening ahead. I climbed into bed that night still feeling anxious, and processing the events that had occurred intermittently throughout the course of that day and the week.

I kept repeating internally, "*If I don't feel better tomorrow then I will take the day off from the gym and just relax.*"
Seemed like a good plan.

But, as you know in life, things rarely go to plan and this would change dramatically the following morning. When I woke up, I felt ok. It wasn't until I placed my feet on the floor to physically get out of bed and walk to the bathroom that would render me speechless. I was physically unable to lift my left leg any higher than maybe a couple of centimetres. It was like it was made of concrete all over again, only this time it wouldn't move at all. I tried three or four times to make it "work" but couldn't raise it any further. By this stage, my anxiety levels were sky high.
I cautiously stood up. Once again, confusion set in as I began to take a step and realised I could walk on it. It didn't make any sense. I could walk on it but not lift it? My brain was now in overdrive as to what was occurring.

I cautiously made my way to the bathroom and changed into my gym gear, proceeded into the kitchen to prepare my usual morning greens drink and take my supplements. As I stirred the powder in the glass, I kept silently stressing about the events that had just taken place. Whilst these thoughts were spinning in my head, the next event would occur. I placed the glass down on what I thought was the cutting board, but again, misjudged it and placed it on the edge.

The glass immediately tipped over and thick green liquid spilled over the kitchen bench, down the cupboard doors, under the kettle and toaster and onto the floor. I burst into tears thinking, " *What is happening to me!?"*

My ex had been a first responder for over 20 years and had witnessed some horrendous accidents and situations. It was around 8am when I made the call, bursting into a flood of tears once more, whilst simultaneously explaining everything that had happened over the course of that week. Anyone who knows me understands that if I am crying, I'm either overjoyed or something serious is taking place. I knew what he was going to say before he even spoke.

"It's ok. It sounds neurological. Like your brain can't communicate properly to the body. I think you should go to Emergency and have it checked out. Do you want one of us to take you or do you want to call an ambulance now?"

I chose to wait for his then partner to arrive and collect me, as he was taking Chanel to school. Both of us agreed she needed to have her morning routine as normal as possible in the short term until I had answers.

That morning was a blur of events. I lost count of the hours spent waiting in the Emergency Department, still unable to lift my leg yet still able to walk on it. I had hourly blood pressure tests, doctors coming in and out, me repeating my story over and over, again and again and yielding the same perplexed looks on their faces trying to piece together what it could possibly be. Different ward doctors, different nurses repeating how fit and healthy I looked, how upbeat my spirits were, that all my vitals were perfect, so other than the leg, none of them could understand logically what was happening either.

It wasn't until I was wheeled away for a full CT scan and wait a further 4 hours for the results, that I would receive the life changing news and diagnosis.

Each challenge in life is building character, resilience, patience, strength and will power to overcome future obstacles and most likely, to help others you meet along the way. These challenges and major life events are also mostly to prepare you for what you asked for, or for what you are **DESTINED** for.

None of us are born ready for these challenges and traumas. As with school, we all must learn the lessons, do the tests, pass or fail, often having to re-sit the exam over and over until we learn the master lessons, or progress onwards and upwards to the next grade.

And let me tell you, these levels will have a whole new set of devils - spiritually, mentally and physically. It is, in essence, similar to playing the real life version of Jumanji.

Life's tests can and will, also come from forces beyond the realms that do not want you to know how powerful you truly are. Like missiles sent from a submarine they are intentionally launched to destroy your spirit, create blocks, stops or distractions, blow things up or keep you stuck in low vibrational energy, old thought patterns, toxic relationships, unworthiness, self-sabotage, and fear.
All to prevent you from R-I-S-I-N-G.

These defining moments in life are sometimes sent by the enemy, to attack your weaknesses and vulnerability to prevent and restrict you from becoming the magnificent human that you are. Psychic attacks and different forms of spiritual warfare are very, very real. Now more than ever. These can also come through family, friends, work situations, random strangers or unexplainable events around you, so be aware.
If you are a lightworker or have been chosen for a specific spiritual mission to help humanity, then let me just say, some adversities will be sent to literally TAKE YOU OUT.
Indefinitely.

I was once given the phrase, *"the bigger the storm, the bigger the purpose."*
On many occasions, I would jokingly say, *"Well I must be destined for big things!"* Maybe my higher self was giving me a preview of future events? Of

course, in the reality-soaked present moment that evening, I wished I could grab my higher self and instead say, "*Seriously.. Is this what I signed up for?!*"

You will know when it is from God and when it is not. God will send the rainbow after the storm. Every single time. I did not believe this until I truly began to pay attention and understand the bigger picture playing out and the process I had to go through. No matter what you are struggling with at this moment, you are just in the process. And everybody will have to endure their own winters as they go through life. Some will be bigger than others but endure them just the same. Some will be intense but very short-lived. Others will have less intensity, but over longer periods. Some will have a mix of both. In those moments, it is not the end.

Everything has an expiration date.
Everything.

It may take only hours or days. Sometimes it may continue for weeks, months, or even years, but eventually it will come to an end. Somehow and some way. Everything is always in a perpetual state of change. The winds will, and do, eventually blow in another direction.
In other words, the more trials and challenges that life has you endure, most likely the higher the calling.

However - not everyone that is chosen will accept the assignment.

If your destiny is centred around greatness and influence, then your soul is calling you to be of service to humanity. If that is the case, be prepared for significant setbacks, major resistance, full blown distractions and surprise situations that may cause you to feel as though your world is self-destructing around you.

You are either being attacked or tested.
Broken down or rebuilt.

Ask yourself how you are feeling about the situation you are facing right now. Does it feel like you are under attack?

Or do you intuitively sense that perhaps your current giant is more like a giant test?

Remember, David beat Goliath with a slingshot and a stone.

Just because it looks bigger and more formidable than you, doesn't mean it will BEAT you.

Looks can be very deceiving.

If you sit in the silence long enough the answer will always come.

We all have an inbuilt GPS or, as some like to call it, an IGS – Inner Guidance System.

Tapping into it can simply be done by meditating or taking a few deep breaths, clearing your head, and then asking yourself your question. The first answer that pops into your head will usually be the right one and coming from your S-O-U-L. To confirm, if you feel good about it, a sense of calm or confidence or clarification, then you are tapped into your IGS!

If your stomach churns and turns or you feel anxious or second guess your answer, then most likely you are not grounded enough in that moment or it is your intuition telling you - NO, wait, or that perhaps further information or clarification is required.

It is in these moments of absolute destruction that you must dig deep into the reserves of your soul and find what feels like your last piece of inner strength and resolve to RISE to the challenge.

One of the most profound statements I've ever heard was:

> **You will never know how much you can handle until you are in it.**
> **Hashtag - #TRUTH**

When you are in the storm it is easy to feel as though you are being tossed around, anxious, unbalanced, scared, uncertain, lost. The storm will pass. Stay anchored. Stay in faith that you are being protected and guided. Stay strong. It may feel like all hell is breaking loose, and it probably is, however nothing endures forever.

Everything has its time. Storms do not last. They can be fierce and destructive. There may be complete carnage, bucketful's of tears, scratches, bruises and losses - sometimes devastating losses, but life goes on and you will come out the other side. Everything may be falling away around you. You may be completely stripped bare of people, places and things that were once so precious, so loved, so valuable – or maybe just plain old comfortable - but you will be OK.

> **".....Spirit is above you, below you, in front of you and behind you, all of the time.... You are never alone."**

MIRACLE INSPIRATION: Begin your battles on your knees. Always. In other words - PRAY.

When you are faced with a storm, call on God/Spirit/Source/Divine Creator/ Universe – however you reference the Almighty Higher Power - FIRST.
In the storm, God never said he would save the boat.
He said He would save YOU.

Ask your guides and angels to help guide you through whatever it is you're facing.
They are always with you and just waiting for you to ASK.
Remember – they see everything. But they cannot interfere in FREE will unless you ASK.
And most of all, while you are waiting for the storm to pass and things to change: KEEP GOING!

Keep doing.
Keep believing.
Keep praying.
Keep persevering.
Keep trusting.
BUT DO NOT GIVE UP.
NEVER.
EVER.

Make this statement non-negotiable. There is no Plan B. Only Plan A. In my case, this was literally my action plan. True story.

And if you are praying, and the situation isn't changing, then maybe the Divine Creator is using the situation to change YOU.

Or perhaps it is to change the people who are around you and watching you. Perspective.

....

> "A single event can awaken within us a stranger totally unknown to us." ~ Antoine de Saint-Exupery

....

Chapter 3

GET EDUCATED – KNOW YOUR DEMON

· ·

"I also believe that when people are going through difficult situations in life… it causes them to search a lot more. They search life and search their soul. When you're searching, you're suddenly a lot more open to the world around you, to the possibilities, to things you never thought about before. — When you're happy, you don't question the world so much. When you're lost, you question everything. The very reason why it is so essential to human self-discovery." ~ Cecelia Ahern

· ·

Deactivate the charge behind the diagnosis, the life event, the adversity.

Hard to do when you are smack bang in the midst of a life-changing diagnosis, inconsolable grief or a major life crisis right?

In my case, nearly ten hours is a long time to contemplate life, think about a gazillion scenarios and it was a long time to put my Gemini Google mind into full *"just figure it out"* mode.

In the lead up to the final result that eventful evening, I had begun researching what I *"thought I had"*, basically self-diagnosing with 25 years of health and wellness experience.

In that time, I had narrowed it down to two highly possible scenarios - a blood clot or a mini stroke. I laugh and shake my head when I reflect on this now. How completely wrong I was. But strangely, I had already accepted the high likelihood of either, given the sudden unexplainable symptoms that had landed me in this situation. After all, it made perfect sense, given a heart history on my father's side, my biological age, a shooting pain on and off in my left elbow in the weeks leading up to this day (I assumed was a gym injury), the inability to lift my left leg higher than a couple of centimetres, the neurological signs of missing the water bottle with my hand driving in the car and the miscalculations that morning on the simple task of picking up a glass and placing it on the cutting board in the kitchen.

As I read and researched, the hours waiting seemed to endlessly drag on. I began to ACCEPT and make peace with these possibilities. Logically, I concluded it couldn't be that bad. I was still here. Nothing major had happened. I felt oddly uncomfortable yet also more relaxed as both just made sense. And so, tucked behind the closed curtain of the emergency ward bay that evening, I went within to feel the emotion behind both possible scenarios and release them.

By the time the ward doctor returned, I had already deactivated the energetic and emotional charge around these two options being the actual diagnosis. Both scenarios were fixable and with my background and lifestyle, easily managed. At that moment I was ready for him to tell me what I thought I already knew.

But life as you know, NEVER runs the way you plan.
EVER.

When big things are happening, it can feel as though your entire world has been tipped upside down and in that present and blinding moment I was as human as the next person, filled to the brim with raw emotions.

Consequently, after being read the cold, hard and incomprehensible truth, I waited for the Ward Doctor to leave, keeping myself together as I always did under stress and pressure, before bursting into a flood of tears. It was a level of shock and grief I had not felt in years.

My mind was racing. I was in sheer disbelief. For those first few minutes everything felt surreal. Time stood still. I felt paralysed. I checked my leg again. I could lift it now. This cannot be right? I could not fathom it being ME. ME... being diagnosed with BRAIN CANCER? Then the monkey mind began throwing out an endless stream of internal questions.

How did I get here? How does this happen? How does this happen to ME? This must be a mistake? Stage 4? Incurable? Inoperable? I cannot die.

What about Chanel? Who will take care of her? How will she cope? I cannot leave her. How do I tell my family? What should I say? How will they handle it? Who do I call? I cannot call anyone. It's too late. How did I not have any earlier symptoms? How have I got to this stage with NOTHING showing up earlier? No headaches? No fatigue? No seizures? No bleeding? No anything? "Why now?" And again, the classic, *"Why ME?"*

After a few minutes of intense tearful, almost hyper-ventilating release, I gathered my thoughts and switched into survival mode. All those traumatic and unexpected tragedies and life events had taught me resilience in spades and how to detach emotionally very quickly. Was this a good thing or a bad thing? I honestly do not know and still cannot decide. But right in that moment it was truthfully what carried me through the rest of that long, exhausting night on my own.

The first task in my head was, *"Who do I call?"* And then, *"What do I even say?" How do I even start this conversation?"*

Jay and Bianca were my initial contact that night. Sixteen years of working together, watching them build successful businesses, birth and raise children, the ups and downs of marriage, and everything in between. Through sharing the good times, the rough times and the tough times, we had developed an extraordinarily strong friendship, almost family ties. Jay would often say I was the sister he never had and to me, it was one of the highest compliments to ever receive from one of the most prominent influencers and mentors in my life.

And in a strange and almost freakish twist of Fate, we had all arranged dinner together that night, joined by other friends. The irony of life. The polarity of the two. One filled with joy and laughter, funny stories, great food and wine. Enjoying life. Enjoying friends. Enjoying the moment. The essence of what was usually an amazing, entertaining and memorable night out. Yet here I was, about to send them what felt like one of the worst-case scenarios ever.

In my head I was processing thoughts of, *"How are they going to handle this?"* My message was short and simple, yet in true Gemini mode, honest, upfront and almost brutal. *"Why sugar coat it? You cannot sugar coat it really. Jay and Bee know me very well. It is black or it's white. There is no in between."* and so, my text message simply read:

"Don't call Jay. I'll just cry.
They've found clusters in the brain and brain bleeds. They're saying it could be cancer. Will be here for the weekend probably. No surgery tonight but given an anti-inflammatory to bring the brain swelling down. Still to speak to another neurosurgeon."

It didn't take long for the reply.

"Holy shit oh my god Kath I don't know what to say? Please know that I'm here for you. Anything you need please call me ASAP. If you are up for a visit tomorrow let me know. We love you hun, stay strong."

Queue more deep, almost inconsolable crying from me.

"I'll be here all weekend probably. They want to do more tests and scans to see if there's any other clusters in the body. It's in the brain on the left side behind the op (operated on) eye."

"I'm speechless. Please don't hesitate to call if you need anything or just want to chat."

"Well Jay, I refuse to accept cancer. I'll alkalise the body, do healings, get CBD oil, get treatments and surround myself with people who love me and have my back."

"Have you got anyone with you now?"

"No. But my ex is meant to be coming back in. Probably Chanel will stay with his partner."

"Do you want some support? I'm happy to come up?"

"Thank you. You know I'll cry. Already had my head around a stroke or clot, not this. Anyway, a full body scan hopefully tomorrow. Not accepting anything until I have all the tests back. They're taking more blood shortly."

"Honestly, please, if you want company I will be there in a flash. We can cry together if that helps?"

"F*cking hell Jay. Can you believe this? I'm in shock. Just waiting to hear from him and my sister."

"I just want you to know you will beat this I guarantee you. You are such a strong person and bad shit does not happen to good people. Myself and Bee are crying here Kath. Are you sure you don't want company until he gets there?"

"I'm ok. I've calmed down. Still to be admitted. What do you do? I'm resilient so not accepting anything until I've got all the facts."

"100% Kath. Wait until you have all the info and then come up with a game plan."

It wouldn't be long before the neurosurgeon on duty would visit, explain the immediate next steps and what was ahead of me in the morning.

"Just spoke to the neurosurgeon. They are admitting me under a medical team tonight. The neurosurgeon was amazing. I just said, give it to me straight. So, he did. Two brain bleeds. One smaller one at the back of the neck and the other on the front left side above the eye, forehead area. Not urgent apparently otherwise

I would be on an operating table. More concerned with the clusters. Front of the brain on the left side and side of the head. Did all my tests again and said the anti-inflammatory should bring down swelling and hopefully take pressure off the nerve that's impacting my ability to move my leg. Will do scans tomorrow in sections on my lungs, stomach, kidneys and other organs and an MRI on my brain hopefully. May need to take tissue samples. So basically, I am here until they say otherwise."

"Wow. I'm thinking of you and I'm sure everything will be good. We will come up to see you tomorrow. Just try to get some sleep."

I can honestly say that after the initial bomb went off, it would be 1.30am in the morning before being transferred to the Oncology Ward, given a sleeping tablet and left to rest. One of the longest and most profound days in my entire life. And believe me, I've had a few.

When I woke the following morning, it was almost as if time had frozen, as I grappled with the initial shock and emotions of the situation all over again. The constant influx of medical checks, interventions and medications, solidifying the severity of it all. Everything felt surreal, almost as though I was in some kind of dramatic and intense episode of Grey's Anatomy.

I had been blessed with my own private room looking out over a small but quiet courtyard, interlocking two other sections of the hospital.

It was a sunny day, and my first observation was the butterflies amongst the trees outside. Thank goodness I had some greenery and nature to look at to maintain a sense of calm and groundedness. I smiled at the butterflies and said a little "*thankyou*" as they had always spiritually represented my guides and angels were with me.

I began repeating internally this can't be true. It just can't be. I kept watching the door, saying over and over in my mind, "*Surely any minute now, a doctor will walk in and say they have made a terrible mistake and it was a misdiagnosis and I can go home."*

Nurses would enter and exit the room routinely to constantly check my temperature and blood pressure and fuss around me. I was immediately placed on what felt like a pharmacy of medication.

When the Oncologist on shift finally arrived and confirmed what had been detected in the scans, I felt almost nauseated. It wasn't only predominently in the brain, but also found in the lungs and detected in the left hip/rump area, having metastasised silently from somewhere in the body and spreading through the lymph glands.
I was to discover months later that it was found heavily through both lungs, as well as the pelvis, left hip/rump, bowels and of course, the brain.

More fun times.

After his routine patient visit and the obvious conversation around what would happen next, I was left in silence and solitude to process his words. Here I was sitting in a hospital bed in the Oncology Ward on a beautiful, warm Saturday morning. It felt so unbelievable and inconceivable, almost as though I was in a bad movie. And I was.

Thoughts of Chanel and the impact on her immediate life filled my mind as did thoughts on how family and friends would handle it. In that raw and very real space I wondered what to say, how to tell them, how does everything work and how does life and everything around this get handled moving forward?

Feelings of overwhelm consumed my body. My head was spinning with a hundred different questions and scenarios. I could feel my body tensing up, waves of anxiety and disbelief surging through me. Then, almost out of nowhere, I'm sure it was my angels and divine soul team, I felt a strong surge of inner determination, strength and grit from deep inside, completely wash over me.

It was almost as if a switch turned on, and my brain and mindset shifted to *"Stop it. Listen, get over it. This isn't achieving anything. Little children and elderly people are going through this. This happens to thousands of people around the world every single day. You are not the only one. So let's get on with it. Handle it a thousand different ways but handle it. This is just a test and is not going to beat you."*

Somewhere in those first few hours I kept feeling this profound sense of determination, inner strength and probably a good dose of stubbornness washing over me. In those defining moments that morning, it was as though my higher self gave me an inner slap on the face and said, *"Right. Day one. This is the cards you have been dealt, so what are you going to do about it?" You can either sit here and feel sorry for yourself and hate the world for dishing out such a shitty situation, or you can put yourself back in control and focus on what CAN be done."*

So I did.

My driving force that Saturday morning was, and still is, my gorgeous divine daughter. I found my warrior spirit and called on God/Spirit/Source/Creator, my guides, angels, my ancestors and family in Heaven and said *"You see what is happening. You knew this was coming. This is not a surprise to you. Obviously, you have allowed this for a reason. I don't understand why you are allowing this, so I need your help and healing and guidance. I know you have got this. I TRUST you."*

"God gives His toughest battles to His strongest warriors."

At that moment I took a few deep breaths, let go of the outcome, HOW it would happen and the usual monkey mind of WHEN. I gave it all to God and knew this was given to me for a reason. And if it was given to me for a reason then there must be a bigger purpose. And if there was a bigger purpose then I had to persevere through it. No matter what. The purpose would reveal itself in time.

As my brain began to shift into this new perspective, I thought, *"well Kath, this is where you walk your walk sweetheart. No more talking. You cannot change it right now. It's already here. Everything you have been preaching about health and wellness for decades and in training for, is right in front of you. If you were ever going to be tested this is it. So, let's see what you got."*

And whether it was delayed shock or a coping mechanism learnt from childhood to literally "switch off", from that moment forward, I continued to focus on changing my perspective, and viewing it as a life test not a death sentence. Because it wasn't, and isn't. And so began this unbelievable journey of twists and turns, filled with tears at times, but filled with more deep gratitude, support and love from an army of amazing friends, family and strangers.

Shortly afterwards, I was collected for what was to be the beginning of 5 days of further testing, scans, retesting and of course, modifications to the prescribed medications.

As each day passed, I had to fight my own inner self of wanting to go home and simply return to normal. Friends and work crew popped in for visits bringing me everything from food to flowers to cards and gifts. I was deeply touched by their thoughtfulness and beautiful, caring messages, along with some much needed laughter, and lighthearted banter in between.

The nurses were simply amazing. In amongst the chaos I used my negotiating and influencing skills to sneak a few temporary leave passes, allowing me to venture outside and spend some precious time with Chanel, whilst trying to keep her little world as centred and grounded as I possibly could.

To this day I have never directly mentioned the "C" word to her, nor have I ever told her directly what the diagnosis was. In my mind I rationalised that just because this was the situation NOW, it may not be the situation in the coming months ahead, so why worry her?

At that moment, I simply said, *"Mummy's ok sweetheart. I've just got to stay in hospital for a little bit while the doctors do some tests ok".*

I kept reminding myself internally that if I remained calm, she would remain calm. As within, so without. Her little routine continued. School continued. Her father would bring her in almost daily so she could see that mum was ok. I feel this helped her greatly to understand and view with her own innocent little eyes that everything was ok, that mum was fine. She could see I was calm, not distressed. This was my preferred response, rather than mentioning it was cancer and her being unable to understand or process the immediate diagnosis.

Of course, everyone's situation and scenario will be different. I am simply writing my story of how I handled it.

And as the days passed and the tests were done, it became one day closer to going home. That was my very first goal. And let me tell you, I was so grateful and happy and overjoyed the day I left! Home has always been my safe haven, my sanctuary. From that day forward however, it became my fortress and my healing space.

In life, as I've discovered, chaos, distractions, or complete destruction may come from God/Source/Spirit to teach you the master lessons you require for your soul purpose as you progress along your path. Like a parent watching mindfully as their children make mistakes, so too does Spirit. Never giving you more than you can handle at any given time. I remember at the time thinking to myself, *"Are you kidding me right now? Really? This?"*
And again the classic, *"Why me?"*

Remember, Spirit will eventually come along and literally blow things up, usually without any prior warning, to redirect your life and place you back where you are supposed to be. And believe me when I say, you will NOT be ready for it. You will not be prepared. And you certainly will not know what the hell just happened.

You will however, most probably feel like you cannot go on. The towers may have you dropping to your knees in sheer grief, distress and desperation. God will usually isolate you, strip everything bare, burn everything to the ground so you have no other option BUT to do the inner work to heal, whilst He works on your heart and SOUL, to rebuild you from the ground up.

Especially when it's time for you to UPLEVEL.

Taking you sometimes to your absolute breaking point and putting you under almost unbearable, intense pressure like a diamond in the rough, yet lovingly watching you like a parent if you feel overwhelmed, take a wrong turn and wander off your path, or choose a direction that leads to a less than desirable outcome.

I remember reading somewhere once, that when our brain says we cannot cope any longer, we are only operating at 40%. In my mind, even through my darkest days, I kept repeating, *"You still have 60% left in the tank Kath. Keep going."*

Likewise in life, I have learnt over time to never fear - FEAR. You cannot get rid of it. You cannot hide from it. You cannot outrun it. But you can go through it. Why? Because fear is predominantly an INSIDE job. Internally created as a safety mechanism to protect you. However nothing in this world would have been achieved if people did not feel the fear and do it anyway. Fear, at its core, is often described as False Evidence Appearing Real. So here I was, literally on the edge of the precipice with the only option being to jump. In FAITH. Full complete faith that no matter what happened in the freefall I would be caught.
Eventually.
This was not the end.
It was just the beginning.

I began researching. Geminis in general have curious minds and usually an unquenchable thirst for knowledge, so this felt easy to me. With my extensive background in health and wellness, I was also intuitively aware of the information I was searching for. Ultimately this was the beginning of making peace with the demon I was dealing with.

I detached from OWNING it. Because I didn't own it. Any of it. In any of its forms. In my eyes it was like an intruder in my home, only it was intruding in my body. It had snuck in like a thief in the night, infiltrating, hijacking and changing my healthy cells. My body had been silently under siege and at war internally without any prior warning.
Hence, from that moment forward I referred to the clusters in the brain as "snowflakes" not cancer cells. As for the ones in the body, I chose to completely ignore them, as the doctors seemed to be ignoring them too, visualising them disappearing or returning to normal healthy cells.

I never once took OWNERSHIP of the diagnosis I was given.
I never attached it to ME.

To the best of my knowledge I didn't verbalise or repeat, *"I have brain cancer."*
Instead I consciously reworded phrases to, *"They've said it is ...."* or *"The diagnosis was ...."* or *"I am in the process of healing from... ... "*
Where attention goes, energy flows. Again, this was a conscious CHOICE.

Food for thought - what language are you using to describe your current challenge and are you unconsciously owning it?

I intentionally set my vision on shifting my focus, my words, my thoughts and my ENERGY, choosing to manifest HEALING only and I cover this in another chapter.

There is undeniable metamorphosis in the dark. Battles are usually fought and won in the dark. And usually in solitude and silence. Imagine for a moment, the proverbial seed being planted. Buried so deeply underground. Imagine the pressure of the dirt, the darkness, the length of time gestating, and the sheer level of RESISTANCE that the tiny seed must undergo to finally push through and reach sunlight. If you are currently in the midst of a challenge, then perhaps YOU are the seed, being transformed under pressure to push through the resistance. This is where solid, lasting GROWTH occurs.

There will always, always, always, be a much higher purpose for the pain. You decide, however, whether to look at it as a negative experience and focus on the bitterness, anger, resentment or the classic, WHY ME?

That was the old me.
All things made manifest.

Or whether you choose the POSITIVE experience, regardless of how small that may seem right now – the personal growth, the added resilience, the increased strength and, of course, the personal life experience and empathy to help guide and lift others through similar challenges.

Where you may see darkness, others may see LIGHT.

MIRACLE INSPIRATION: Live like a WARRIOR so you can die like a LEGEND.

Give it all you got.
Know what you are dealing with.
Get educated. Research. Then research some more.
Follow your own Inner Guidance System.
Your higher self already knows the answers.

· ·

"I have realised; it is during the times I am far outside my element that I experience myself the most. That I see and feel who I really am, the most! I think that's what a comet is like, you see, a comet is born in the outer realms of the universe!

But it's only when it ventures too close to our sun or to other stars that it releases the blazing "tail" behind it and shoots brazen through the heavens! And meteors become sucked into our atmosphere before they burst like firecrackers and realise that they're shooting stars!

That's why I enjoy taking myself out of my own element, my own comfort zone, and hurling myself out into the unknown.

Because it's during those scary moments, those unsure steps taken, that I am able to see that I'm like a comet hitting a new atmosphere: suddenly I illuminate magnificently, and fire dusts begin to fall off of me! I discover a smile I didn't know I had, I uncover a feeling that I didn't know existed in me... I see myself. I'm a shooting star. A meteor shower. But I'm not going to die out. I guess I'm more like a comet then. I'm just going to keep on coming back."

~ C. JoyBell C.

WRITE THE END AT
THE BEGINNING –
MANIFESTING A MIRACLE

Make a CLEAR and concise statement of what you desire and what you
BELIEVE

....

"Think the thought until you believe it, and
once you believe it, it is." – Abraham Hicks

....

After my first post-hospital MRI, the rather daunting results were explained,
showing there were 15 "snowflake" clusters scattered throughout the brain,
all different sizes and apparently aggressively growing. I often say to people,
touch your head 15 times in different spots. That will give you an accurate
understanding of what I was initially presented with. Not including the body.
Unfathomably, other people's diagnoses can be far worse.

That day, I remember walking into the kitchen, turning the results papers
over and writing my desired intention on the back page. At the time I was
so determined and committed to ignoring what the report said and instead,
was hell bent on scripting my own medical notes!

On the 14th of March 2021, I penned these statements on the back of the report:

'I am so grateful and thankful and blessed now that these clusters are all completely healed and gone, never to return anywhere in my body.
My body functions at pure divine perfect health and wellness.
I AM HEALTHY, WHOLE and WELL. I feel amazing!
In divine perfect timing and for my highest good by July 2021.
And so it is. Amen."

I wrote a clear and concise intention, I felt it with every fibre of my being, placed it under my manifesting pyramid, and released it to God and the universe. Ironically it was the fourteenth. The number fourteen is my birthdate and my daughter's birth date. It has followed me through life and constantly shows up around people, places and situations.

Of course, it is powerful to timestamp it. However, the Creator always knows the most perfect divine time for YOU. Initially there was slight disappointment that my manifestation didn't eventuate in that timeframe, however I knew deep in my soul it would happen suddenly and when I least expected it. I anchored into my faith once more and accepted that that is how the Divine works. God's timing. Not mine.

Looking back, I now see WHY it didn't happen my way. There would be more epiphanies. More inner work to do. More healing. More people to help, inspire and encourage along the way. There would be added strength and determination to handle the shitty bits and of course, more leaning in to trust and faith than ever before.

This book was in fact delayed multiple times and was nine months over what I originally intended! Metaphorically, it honestly felt as though I was birthing another baby. However, the universe ALWAYS knows the perfect time. Mostly, that perfect time won't be OURS. Reflecting now, it was all by design. There was a great deal more that needed adding, revising and re-wording. I continually received downloads, messages and confirmations on what was to be included or taken out, as well as bittersweet tributes to some beautiful people who were taken too soon. Not to mention the spiritual warfare sent to block, stop, distract and delay my progress.

In the midst of our challenges, when things aren't going the way we want, or we don't get what we THINK we deserve, need, or have asked for, there will ALWAYS be a reason for the delay, the detour or the set back. This may be revealed in the future or not at all.
Just know that all delays aren't denial.
Setbacks might just be set UPS.
And no doesn't always mean it's the end, perhaps simply, NOT RIGHT NOW.

It is one thing to THINK something, but when we WRITE it out, all the powers and energy behind those words are activated and released.
Where intention goes, energy flows. Our FEELINGS are the key. When we are writing, we are CREATING and feeling our desired outcome. These emotions are amplifying the energy behind the intention. It is flowing through you, into your hand and out onto the paper.

This is also true for the SPOKEN word and I will expand on this later. However, there is vast power in the written word. Write AS IF it has already happened.
Be precise. Get detailed. Write how you want to FEEL. How your manifestation looks. How it will positively impact your life or those around you. Write dates, amounts or whatever it is you are wanting to manifest into reality and be as specific as you can. The more you write with feeling and intention, the more in alignment you become with it.

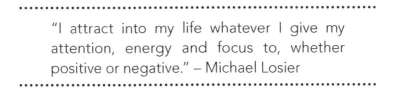

"I attract into my life whatever I give my attention, energy and focus to, whether positive or negative." – Michael Losier

Celebrate small wins along the way! Even though I did not receive exactly what I had written and hoped for on that date, the following MRI conducted at the end of May, had yielded more positive results!

Kathryn Mills

"Your radiation to the brain was highly successful. All of them have shrunk considerably in size. There is no new activity. Some have completely disappeared off the scan. You have a small hole in the brain where one of the larger ones used to be and another that looks as though it is going in that direction. Fantastic result."

After relaying the positive news, Jim's tone automatically shifted, admitting the initial scans were grim, indirectly implying he gave me little hope of staying alive given the severity and growth in the brain and body. I may not have manifested my exact intention, however with such positive results it was headed in the right direction.

I believe that day, he was also witnessing the beginning of a miracle in motion.

And whilst my complete healing journey is still in progress, I know God, my angels and guides have got this. So why worry? It's not my job to know the how, when, where and why. This is the part where many of us get caught out. We trip ourselves up with EXPECTATIONS, playing the movie reel in our minds of how WE want things to go, the time frame and every detail in between. We imagine all kinds of scenarios and when it doesn't happen how we want, or when we want, or things go backwards, or blow up, this is where stress, frustration, anger, disappointment, grief and a mixed bag of other emotions will surface. Essentially, we are trying to tell God, Source, Spirit, HOW to do everything.

Do your part and God will do His – when the time is right.

That's why He is God, and you are not. His ways are far better than our ways. Imagine your desired manifestations are a Rubix cube. To bring them into existence, it is not just one square that has to be aligned – but ALL of them. There are other people, places, things and situations that have to be aligned FIRST - before the entire cube comes together. On the outside, it may appear as though nothing is happening or working out how you want. In fact everything may look a complete and utter mess, yet behind the scenes, Spirit is silently and strategically working on realigning, recalibrating or repositioning other people and parts of your story to bring your manifestation, or wish, to fruition.

Be patient.

Not only is writing down your desired intentions a powerful manifestation technique, it is also a wonderful opportunity to allow your creativity and unique expression to come to LIFE. There are numerous manifesting experts who practise, teach (or taught) and endorse this technique, including some of my favourites - Joe Dispenza, Wayne Dyer, Bob Proctor, and Louise Hay, to name just a few. That is (or was) their domain, their gift and life purpose. I am simply guiding you in a similar direction.

Always take what lands in your soul and leave the rest. I encourage you to follow your own path and intuition and allow yourself to be guided to the perfect mentors for YOU.
I keep saying, I am just the messenger. A spiritual conduit through which information is delivered and seeds are planted for others to go pursue, investigate, research, contemplate or to take action themselves.
That is where YOUR power lies. The journey of self-discovery is a powerful journey. Everyone will be different.

MIRACLE INSPIRATION: Write as if your desired result has already manifested.

"I AM so grateful and thankful and blessed now that I AM completely healed. I AM healthy and I AM whole. Every cell in my body resonates in divine perfect health."

This can be for anything you desire a positive or specific outcome for.
I encourage you to write down 3 things at this moment that you would love to manifest.
I prefer to do this on separate pages in a journal or single pieces of paper.

Once you have written them down, now begin to get specific and detailed with each one. Write WHY you want to manifest your desired intention.

••

"Ask for what you want and be prepared to get it." – Maya Angelou
••

I AM so grateful and thankful and blessed now that my body is completely healed and whole and vibrating in perfect divine health.

Every day, I AM so happy and grateful for my perfectly healthy body. I AM blessed with a long, prosperous and successful life to enjoy and watch my beautiful daughter grow into a confident, strong, successful and independent woman. My body is strong, fit and powerful, enabling me to continue enjoying simple things such as quality time with my daughter, driving my car, enjoying nature, the beach, staying active, catching up with friends, the ability to work with ease and flow, helping humanity and doing what I love. I AM so grateful for feeling vibrant, happy and at peace living in my favourite location by the beach. I AM full of energy and every day is a gift.
I AM always taken care of because life supports me in every way.
Each day is a blessing.

Remember, we cannot change or alter the past, but we can create and manifest a beautiful future.

....

> "You manifest what you believe, not what you want." – Sonia Ricotti

....

Chapter 5

DO NOT ACCEPT THE STATUS QUO – SHIFT YOUR PERSPECTIVE

. . . .

"The body is a self-healing organism, so it's really about clearing things out of the way so the body can heal itself." ~ Barbara Brennan

. . . .

Let's begin by backtracking for a moment:

Given the initial round of scans were anything but positive, along with the amount of activity and growth especially in the brain, my immediate daily regime over the first two and half months would include radical high dosage medications including 2 different types of chemotherapy tablets (Mektovi and Braftovi) totaling 12 a day with their own book of side-effects.

My brain oncologist explained that this combination, designed as a fast kill in extreme cases like mine, and mixed with Dexmethasone, a powerful steroid medication to reduce the swelling and inflammation, would hopefully make it possible for me to eventually under-go radiation to the brain. In a nutshell, this was the immediate first and final chance in staying alive.

Jim explained that most patients weren't able to handle these medications at full strength given the vast, and harsh amount of side effects. There was also a chance they may not work at all, given the advanced stage of the clusters in the brain and therefore potentially staring down the barrel of an already bleak outcome.

And let me tell you, it definitely didn't start with rainbows and unicorns at all.

My entire body began to immediately reject the effects of the multitude of tablets being continuously pumped into my bloodstream and organs. Pharmaceuticals had been totally foreign to my body for decades, other than my childhood days with asthma.

The Dexmethasone made my body swell and gain weight. The Mektovi and Braftovi made my skin break out in hot, inflamed, itchy rashes, intensifying at night and ultimately causing major sleep deprivation. At times I would continue scratching until my skin was almost bleeding. In return, I was placed on sleeping tablets short term to counteract the side effects until my body internally calmed down. This vicious cycle would continue on and off over the first few months.

In my quest for alternative options, I discovered refrigerating Moo Goo cream (with MSM) eased the immediate skin inflammation, however it was hit and miss on other occasions. The reprieve would be short-lived for a week or two before the rashes, the intense itching, the red, inflamed skin and sleepless nights would repeat all over again.
My daughter would sleep, completely oblivious to the broken nights of incessant scratching with tears in my eyes out in the kitchen applying Moo Goo, ice cubes or steroid cream to my irritated, angry and inflamed skin. My only wish on those long and tiring nights was to simply shut my eyes and rest. My body was tired. My soul was tired.
And this was just the beginning.

Naturally, our skin is the body's largest organ and the overload of prescription medications was pushing out of my body in a major way.
But I was ALIVE!

I continued quietly repeating that everything else was fixable. Maybe not immediately in those moments, but it could be done. This was simply aesthetics, and so I continued to focus on my own protocols to lessen the severity, knowing none of it was permanent, merely another temporary challenge to navigate through.

The radiation however, was on a whole other level. It would be executed in one hit, over one specific and designated week and consisting of 3 intense rounds. Each session was scheduled every second day and would happen around the middle of April. I was informed because of my age and fitness level I could handle it. Most patients undergo radiation once a week or on a more manageable, tolerable and spread out schedule, however Jim made it known that this would essentially be my one and only chance to potentially survive.
In that instant, this became my second goal.

Through the grace of God I passed. The follow up scans miraculously confirming sufficient shrinkage in cell size and reduction in the inflammation had occurred to proceed.

In the lead up to the radiation, a full facial mould consisting of a hard plastic resin would need to be made and fitted. This would be bolted on to my face, front and back, covered with mesh-style holes like cottage cheese. These tiny holes would allow the radiation beams to be precisely lined up and executed. My mouthpiece was tiny, yet felt like a horse's bit as I was instructed to bite down hard so as to keep my mouth perfectly still whilst the radiation was directed into my skull.

I referred to it as the Hannibal Lector mask.

This was not a pleasant experience at all, as the initial construction was completed in two parts, front and back, then heated and placed directly onto my face and behind my head. As it cooled, it formed an exact mould of my head, face and partially around my neck. And I mean EXACT. As they clamped the bolts together to ensure the mask fitted tightly and correctly,compressing it onto my face to minimise any movement, I felt as though I couldn't swallow or breathe. It was literally like a second skin.

However now, instead of feeling supple, it became hard and extremely uncomfortable.

I became tense.

Anxious.

However, as time passed, my rational mind began to reframe the situation. My attitude transformed from one of anxiousness to empowering thoughts of, "*I am a strong woman. I am fit and healthy and well able. I cannot imagine little children and those in their later years having to go through this.*" This shifted my thought pattern, my emotions and my ability to see that yes, I was living this moment, but everything was ok, I was ok, and everything was under control.

Once the mask was formed and completed, it would be saved and moved to the radiation bunker.

My initial round on the Monday was intense. Clearly anything extreme and out of the ordinary was destined to ignite a fear of the unknown. I felt as though I was in some random science fiction scene as the large lead doors opened and my eyes locked on to the patient table where I would lay. My eyes immediately detected the wall of computer screens above it, the incredible rotation and movement of the machine as they manoeuvred it into place and the sheer size and density of the doors. This was another in-your-face moment, with no opt out button.

I was literally moments away from radiation being directed into my skull and brain.

As I lay there prior to the doors closing, mask on, feeling tense and short of breath, a hefty dose of adrenaline began surging through my body. A few tears began to form at the enormity of what was about to transpire. Only this time, I couldn't hug anyone - or move - or speak - or find comfort. Crying wasn't an option either at this point as the mask made it impossible to wipe away any tears.

I remember thinking, "*well this just sucks, doesn't it?*"

For a few short minutes I froze with fear. This was my brain after all, not a general body part. I had to consciously focus on imagining the machine was a Med Bed – a healing bed – and that my guides and angels were in the room with me, and everything would be ok. As I gazed up to the ceiling, I noticed red marker points strategically placed and realised this would be where the beams would be emitted from.

The radiologists in the control room assured me I was in great hands and to essentially lie as still as I could for the next 15-20 minutes. My logical mind immediately chiming in, *"Well obviously! Like I want to move and have this hit my brain in the wrong spot!"*

From the moment the machine was activated, I immediately felt heat on my skull, lines of heat, like someone was drawing on my head and face with a hot marking pen. Warm enough to make you feel it, yet not too hot as to get burnt. As the treatment progressed, I was turned and rotated to specific markers on the machine, in the room and on the ceiling. Literally military precision. A strong, metallic odour began to fill the entire space, lingering in the air until it was all I could smell and taste.

I continued silently praying and giving thanks to God and the angels – specifically Archangel Michael – for being in the room with me, for watching over me, directing the radiologists with pin-point accuracy and for protecting me.

The initial session would be over quickly yet seemed like an absolute eternity. The after care nurses informed me I may experience headaches, fatigue, nausea and could quite literally be sick. As the afternoon progressed into evening, I began to experience the most intense and extreme headaches of my entire life, feeling as though my brain was literally "on fire", like a fierce blazing inferno from the after-effects and beginning of what is known as die off.

These after-effects were combined with the constant compression on both sides of my skull as though it was being squeezed together in a vice. I didn't sleep. At all. It would be one of the worst times throughout this journey that I can vividly remember. The extreme burning sensation inside my brain would continue through the following day, with the pressure and intensity only gradually subsiding that evening. All I could think about was returning to that room to repeat the entire process again the following day.

Fuck.

I prayed again.

The second round on Wednesday, however, would be better. More relaxed. I had a beautiful girlfriend accompany me for support and any after care if it became too much for my body. I prepared myself, listened to the nurse's advice and took a pain reliever prior to the session, to off-set the extreme headaches. The anxiousness had subsided. I felt more upbeat and cheeky so decided to lighten the mood and seriousness of the situation by having some fun with the radiologists. As I walked into the room I jokingly commented and prayed they weren't suffering from a hangover and had been breathalysed before operating heavy machinery. They all laughed.

Laughter has always been an important part of my personality and it helped raise my spirits and vibe, as well as ease my mind on what was ahead. As I lay on the patient table once again, I began to imagine children and elderly patients experiencing this, with no one in the room and a big scary machine. I kept reminding myself this was a dream run for someone like me. I was physically strong, mentally prepped and understood the entire process.

As the hours passed once the session completed, the pressure and heat inside the brain would again begin dialling up in intensity. Luckily it wasn't as severe, and I managed to sleep a little more that night.

The third and final round on Friday was akin to putting on an old pair of shoes with Jay attending for support, as he and Bianca had done for numerous medical appointments prior. The mask had lost most of its tightness and there happened to be an all-female crew in the control room that day. Not that I had any discrimination, but for me the energy simply felt more caring, nurturing, and compassionate. It was an energy I had prayed for because I knew this was I-T.

There was zero room for error.

And I never wanted to see this room again.

Ever.

It was a definitive time where I truly had to lean into my faith and trust in the Divine that everything was exactly as it should be. That I was meant to be there on that day, at that time, with those radiologists and that all was well. As had been the case throughout my entire journey, I received my divine confirmation quickly. One of the radiologists returned to the room after the session was completed to unbolt the mask and help me from the table, and said, *"We don't normally say this, but that was seriously one of the most accurate sessions we have ever done. We absolutely nailed it."*

I felt this immediate surge of emotion as my entire body lit up in goosebumps as confirmation. All I could say was, *"thankyou, thankyou, thankyou."* Not only expressing my gratitude to her and her colleagues, but to Spirit for taking care of me and reassuring me that everything was ok. As I walked out of that room, I continued to repeat those words under my breath.

It would be nearly 2 weeks later however, that those brief moments of joy and relief would change again. As I walked into the kitchen feeling happy and positive, I ran my fingers through my hair and out the ends. Instead of just a few strands appearing in my palms, I literally had a handful. Not just loose strands, but an entire clump complete with hair follicles. As I ran to look in the bathroom mirror, there staring back at me were the bald patches, right to the scalp. Those closely held tears began to fall once again as reality hit home. This was happening to ME and there was absolutely nothing I could do to stop it.

Leading up to this point, I had escaped the more common side effects. My body had adjusted to the tablets, where other patients had stopped due to adverse reactions, or worse, had tragically passed away from their bodies rejecting them. The medications being their last resort in staying alive, therefore I understood and appreciated how incredibly lucky I was.

This was just hair.

Over the course of the following week however, the hair loss intensified. I was scared to brush it, or wash it, or basically touch it, and continued to fall out in my sleep. I would wake to find hair on my pillow every morning over the following weeks and it was completely irreversible and overwhelming.

In describing it to others I would later jokingly say, *"Imagine a 5-year-old taking a mower or a whipper-snipper to your head"*.
Yeh, that.

The radiation had been performed with such precision it left strips down the centre of my scalp, around both ears and over to the back of the head. As it fell out it formed almost perfectly lasered lines with the hair in the middle still intact. I cried and cried. It was like I was losing myself.

As a female, our hair is such a huge part of our feminine make-up. Hair can virtually define us, our personality, the way we look and how others perceive us. We receive compliments on our hair from friends, work colleagues, our partners, family and strangers. We see fabulous hair all over social media and on the red carpet and in magazines. It makes us FEEL good.

Losing my hair was one of the two biggest aspects I dreaded the most going through this entire journey. The other was being unable to drive due to the effects to the brain, concentration, balance and reaction times. Both superficial in the broader scheme of things, yet still deeply impactful in real time. I had vertigo frequently, therefore was unable to lie down or lean forwards or backwards in any capacity, because the pressure in the brain was so intense. This consequently meant having to uber or taxi everywhere, including dropping Chanel to and from school, the gym, my medical appointments, running general errands and completing daily tasks for a solid 3-4 months after the radiation.

At times I wondered what the long term damage to my brain would be, as well as the immediate effects to my ability to ever drive or function normally again. Yet I held the faith it would eventually be ok and trusted in time it would improve.
And it did.
Rather quickly in fact.

Initially the oncologists predicted it may be 6 months of zero driving, possibly longer, if at all. I continued manifesting and praying and doing the work - and the healing - and overcame this hurdle gradually about 4 months after the radiation. In my somewhat rebellious mind, I made a clear concise decision, that I had a child to take care of, work to do and a life to continue living so I was absolutely going to be driving again and it was going to be sooner rather than later.

And whilst the driving was fixable short term, I understood losing my hair was destined to be the bigger challenge mentally.
Hence, following the initial shock and tears, I strengthened my mindset and changed perspective, reminding myself of other cancer warriors, young and old, navigating this superficial, yet challenging territory. I told myself to stop. It's just hair. It will grow back.

Afterwards, I called a girlfriend who was a hairdresser, instructing her to cut off the remainder, both deciding, what was the point in having long bits and no bits all over my scalp?

I won't lie. Initially, I had no other choice but to lean into some serious self-love and self-acceptance catching my reflection in the mirror, almost resembling a badly plucked chicken with tiny tufts of hair in random spots all over my head. I continued anchoring into my heartspace, checking in with my EGO to humbly remind myself this was simply aesthetics. I was ALIVE! Therefore everything else was fixable and not permanent.

Chanel was shocked. I remember her distinctly asking me that evening what had happened to my hair. Her startled little face expressed her complete disbelief and confusion. To keep her emotional state of mind balanced and calm, I simply explained we had cut it all off in the short term because of "the medicine mum was taking", however it would grow back. No big deal. Children are extremely resilient and understanding, and as a parent I feel they could teach many of us a thing or two about SELF-ACCEPTANCE. Whilst she was bewildered and speechless with the sudden change visually, she loved me no matter what.

I decided medical wigs would be the answer as they were almost identical to the style and colour of my own hair, not only to feel good but so society, work colleagues and strangers didn't project the *"oh she's got/had cancer"* energy over me when moving about in public. At no time did I want a stranger's sympathy, or for others to view me any differently. Because I was still ME underneath. I preferred to move about my day, my appointments, school, day-to-day activities, feeling good and blocking any low vibes potentially impacting my healing.

Once the oddness around wearing them disappeared, I began to embrace it and instead focused on the positives. I ultimately saved time each day brushing and styling, money on shampoo, conditioner and other hair care products, valuable time blow drying, as well as the added expense of professional hairdressers cutting and colouring it every 3-4 months. My wigs literally take less than 5 minutes to fit, are always perfect and I never have a bad hair day!

By changing perspective once more, it VISUALLY implanted in my brain and mindset that everything was still normal and ok. Because I could SEE myself with hair in the mirror. I wanted to LOOK how I wanted to BE. It was important to maintain positive momentum and be more up than down, as what you are FEELING is what you are MANIFESTING.

Reflecting on this adjustment phase, I truthfully felt I walked through virtually unscathed compared to thousands of others. Always humbled and always grateful.

I continuously reminded myself that none of this was permanent. If this was the worst it was going to get then toughen up buttercup. Spirit had my back. Therefore, why keep worrying about it. So, to the best of my ability, I didn't. I let it go.

Following this initial period of adapting to my new look, I had to undertake my first full body PET/CT scans since the diagnosis.

To say I was anxious was an understatement. I knew deep down this would set the benchmark for what was to follow, and essentially, where the rubber would meet the road moving forward.

Feeling slightly nervous and with mixed anticipation, I walked into the public oncology room to two new faces. One would be a support coordinator and the other a trainee oncologist. I knew immediately things had improved purely from the absence of my oncologist in the room.

"Your PET/CT scans show a dramatic reduction in strength and activity, the bowels have completely disappeared from the scan (until that moment, I didn't even know I was dealing with the bowels). Both lungs are still present however there has been a reduction in the cell intensity as is the left hip and pelvis."

So, the next stage now is to start you on immunotherapy."

"What does that involve?"

Basically 2.5 hours every 3 weeks and at least 3 to 4 rounds initially".

Sidenote: I had already researched the immunotherapy options.
Bottom line - there were good options that utilised the body's own T-cells, ranging in some countries from $340 000 -$475 000 – yes you read that correctly! and then there were the medically engineered options, with Big Pharma branded brochures brimming with adverse reactions and major organ damage, ranging from $10 000 - $100 000.
Obviously this can vary greatly depending on the country you live in, the public health care scheme and your own level of health insurance.

"I know there are about 3 or 4 different types of immunotherapies for this type of cancer. Is this the one where they boost your T-cells naturally?"

"No. It's a combination of two drugs that will be gradually released through your veins and then slowly filter into your body via a cannula."

"Oh, ok? And what are the side effects?"

"Well, they are the two strongest but most successful combinations of drugs available for these types of melanoma cells."

"But what are the potential side effects?"

After disappearing briefly, the support nurse at that point returned with what looked like a complete booklet as well as an additional print off, with no less than 9 pages of mild to severe side effects, listing virtually all internal organs, including death.
Nice.

I remember sitting there skimming my eyes over the major ones whilst my intuition internally began screaming NO NO NO! I'm sure the look on my face must have said it all, however, I responded with a simple, *"No thanks. I'll pass."*

Both the trainee oncologist and support nurse were rather shocked.

"Don't you understand this is a $50 000 treatment? This is the latest available for this type of cancer and the next step in your plan. These drugs must also be mixed together on the day. You cannot simply change your mind and cancel."

"Yes, and I said no thank you. You can give them to someone else. I would rather take my chances in the interim with the meds I am on until I have done further research and seek a second opinion. I appreciate you have a job to do however thousands of people every day around the world heal from this. There is not just one way."

"But you have a little daughter."

I could feel my heart nearly burst as she spoke those words, almost like a knife to the heart, and I wanted to cry, but I didn't. I held it together.

"I am very well aware of my personal situation and what I am dealing with. It is still a no. This is my body and with 9 pages of side effects and no guarantee of what I may or may not get, it is also my body having to deal with these potential side effects whilst raising my daughter and trying to work at the same time."

"Do you understand what the alternative is?"

"Yes, I know full well the seriousness. No offence, but have you ever had cancer?"

"No?"

"Well then, you are probably not the person to be telling me what I should and should not be doing."

Her face changed. I could see the frustration and disbelief in her eyes. She left the room.
I stood my ground.
It wasn't that I wanted conflict at all.
On the contrary.

Reflecting on that day, what I needed was probably a little comfort and reassurance and probably a better explanation to be honest.
I understood she was simply fulfilling her job description as was the registrar, nonetheless, in an Oncology Ward there needed to be more compassion and understanding. The trainee oncologist sat there slightly dumbfounded by what had transpired. I reiterated to him once more that I understood this was part of their job, however I wouldn't be making a decision until I sought another opinion and conducted my own research.

Never let anyone in the medical field, or those around you, try to push you, or pressure you, into anything that does not sit right internally, or that you feel you need more time to investigate, research or seek second, third or fourth opinions.
Obviously, this was the standard procedure and the tick in the box for "this diagnosis". I felt as though I was on some kind of cancer conveyor belt being moved along to the next stage.
No thanks.

I was to learn a little later from my seasoned oncologist that (based on his professional experience), patients who proceeded with the treatment, generally had a 50% chance of success and a 50% chance of it ending with severe adverse reactions such as diabetes or hospitalisation from mild to severe liver damage. With a 50% chance I was not about to take that gamble on my life. My decision aligned with what I felt best for my body. If you are currently in this situation, I highly encourage you to do your research and follow what you feel is best for YOU.

Not long after that conversation, I had a male member in the gym approach me randomly and ask, *"Are you the girl with brain cancer?"*

My expression likely portrayed the initial shock of being taken completely off guard. As I collected my thoughts on how to respond, I simply said, *"Yes and no. I was diagnosed in February but I am fine thank you."*

He replied, *"I have metastasized melanoma cancer also. What do they have you on?"*

"Mektovi and Braftovi. Why?"

His next question virtually shocked me. *"Did you do the immunotherapy?"*

"No. I refused to have it. I am not prepared to wage my life on a 50% chance that it will work."

"Well I had it and it nearly killed me. I ended up in hospital with major damage to my liver. I was on the verge of needing a liver transplant. I would never do it again."

Whilst remaining poker-faced at his statement and continuing to engage in further small talk, his response internally solidified my choice. I knew it was yet again another confirmation and message from above that I was in fact being looked after, guided and tapped into my intuition.
We proceeded to chat a while longer before I left him with a few words of strength and inspiration.

A similar situation would occur seven months later at a routine three monthly MRI scan. In the lead up, I had been feeling off, my head simply didn't feel right, vertigo would come and go, balance was not exactly perfect.

My intuition was pushing me to go earlier than scheduled (roughly 3 weeks earlier) and so I listened.

Again, I felt strongly it was more die off, however the monkey mind was also having its turn and creating a 3D anxiousness that maybe things weren't right. What if?

On the day I gave it all to Spirit, my guides and angels and made peace with the outcome. I said to myself that this day has already been and gone. My future self has already been before me. Therefore, regardless of the outcome, there was no point worrying about it. Whether it was a positive or negative result, I would accept it and know that everything was exactly how it should be at this moment and I was exactly where I was meant to be at this time.

I remember laying on the machine feeling slightly claustrophobic. This was a brand new machine, the latest technology, but man, was the tunnel low and tight! To top it off, the fibreglass frame was placed and fitted over my face. For a fleeting moment, it brought back memories of the radiation sessions with the Hannibal Lector mask as well as old emotions of anxiety and nervousness. Again, I continued repeating to myself, *"you've been here before Kath, you know exactly what is about to happen. Relax."*

As they turned the machine on, I gradually slid backwards, once again lying there listening to sounds similar to bathroom renovations. I had jokingly described it to friends as jackhammers, drills and hammers around your head. Basically a construction crew in your ears. If you're not a fan of loud noises then this is not your gig!

I won't lie. There were a few tears for a fleeting moment as the monkey mind switched to the humanness and rawness of it all that this could in fact, go either way. Nevertheless, I grounded my energy and brought my attention back to being in a state of complete gratitude. I was still alive, still walking, still at home with my daughter, still active, still working (albeit slightly differently) and still living my life without any
major restrictions.

The scans came and went, with the follow up appointment booked two days later, to discuss the results with my private brain oncologist, Jim.

Walking into the waiting room, I discovered they were running behind with appointments and so, had time to centre myself, calm my nerves and come into a place of peace with whatever the outcome was.

When my name was finally called, I felt good as I stepped into his consultancy room with an open mind and attitude.

It was short, sharp and fast. I literally think I was in there for five minutes. I remember walking through his office door, exchanging the usual small talk, quickly followed by *"So how are the scans looking?"*

Jim replied with words to the effect of, *"Your brain is looking amazing. How's the immunotherapy going?"*

And THAT ladies and gentlemen, is where the entire conversation and body language shifted.

As previously mentioned, I had refused the immunotherapy. Therefore, the results were based entirely on three months of continued meds combined with my own intuitive healing modalities and supplements.

To say Jim's voice and conversation changed DRAMATICALLY is an understatement. It went from happy and relaxed to stern and serious, followed by rather matter of fact statements along the lines of:

"What do you mean you're not doing the immunotherapy? Don't you know you've got a 1 in 10 chance of survival without it? Kathy you are young, healthy and have a little daughter."

Those words hit me like a punch to the stomach. I took a deep breath, grounded my energy and calmly replied:

"Yes, I am well aware of what I do and don't have Jim, however, as I stated previously, I have heard good and not so good reports on it. I am not saying I will not have it but right now I am wanting to get all my scans, tests and results back. I want to have a full body analysis so I can make an informed decision on what I do next."

I remember he almost shook his head in disbelief and once again reiterated the fact that I would have a 1 in 10 chance of surviving.

In my mind I was thinking, I cannot believe he just said that! Who says that to their patients! Any wonder people hear these statements from their specialists or doctors and BELIEVE them, and as such, like a self-fulfilling prophecy, they actually come true!

WORDS ARE POWERFUL.
And words can be CURSES and CONTRACTS over another.
So much so, I have dedicated an entire chapter to this alone.

In that split second, I refrained myself once more and calmly stated, *"I appreciate that you have my best interests at heart Jim and again, I haven't said that I won't do the immunotherapy but again, I want to wait until I have all my results back."*

"So you're still on the tablets then?"

"Yes I am."

"So you've been on them 6 or 7 months now?"

"Yes that's correct."

"Well they've basically done their job now and will most likely stop working."

"Yes I understood from the start that they were a fast kill and a short term fix."

As he sat at his desk, he began hastily scribbling what would be my next MRI referral to be scheduled in 3 months. As he handed it over, I was still in slight disbelief as to the words he had spoken. I wondered whether this was the standard procedure in oncology wards and specialist suites around the world. Automatically speaking NEGATIVE words and worst case scenarios over patients that then stuck in their psyche like tar, attaching energetically to their body and mind, then ultimately M-A-N-I-F-E-S-T-I-N-G in the flesh.

I thanked him graciously for his time and left. Hands on heart, that experience left me rattled for a few days afterwards as I replayed the conversation over in my mind, still shocked and annoyed by his almost chastising tone and the words he had used.

Don't get me wrong, Jim had been amazing in the process of my radiation treatment. And of course, I understood that this was his way of expressing his professional and experienced views. But that is exactly what they were. HIS views based on HIS medical experience.

True, his words as a seasoned specialist carried weight.
But it is not *everyone's* medical experience.
People heal from cancer every single day.
People heal from lots of different illnesses and issues every single day.
MIRACLES happen every single day.

If nothing else that entire brief encounter lit another fire in my belly and fueled my persistence and determination to yield another miraculous result at this next round of full body tests.

The following week, one of the phone enquiries from the office was a young man, similar in age, in his forties. When I called to inquire about his personal reasons behind wanting to invest in one of the company's adjustable beds, his words were, *"It was a skydiving accident. My parachute didn't open properly. I hit the ground from 14 000 feet. I had countless broken bones, 19 fractures, broken pelvis, spinal breaks and have so far endured 23 operations. The doctors told me that surviving was literally one in a million. I shouldn't be alive."*

In my mind I was thinking, *"OMG!!! Who on God's earth survives a skydiving accident from thousands of feet up in the air plummeting to the ground at high speed?!"*

In that moment, I KNEW my guides, angels, God, whoever you believe in, was letting me know that *"sweetheart, if you're time is not up then it's not up and if it is, it is, and so if this man can be the one in a million and survive, then you've so got this."*

I remembered afterwards, intuitively knowing and anchored in the fact that I was meant to speak to this gentleman, and he was meant to tell me his story of not only surviving, but his tenacious resilience, persistence and strength to defeat all the odds and still be alive and standing. Clearly his time on earth was not finished and his gratitude to just wake up in the morning every day and still be here was his biggest blessing and gift from Above.

Bottom line: You need to consciously give yourself permission to stay in victim mode.

The way you perceive not only your immediate situation, but also yourself, is always a choice. This amazing man CHOSE not to be the victim, even though he had every reason and all validation to perceive himself that way.

God, and God alone says when you go and when you stay.

Just ask people who have had near death experiences – or physically died, gone to the other side and been brought back to life. I have personally spoken to a few along my path. Look up the 700Club Interactive on You Tube if you need further validation. And so, if you are still here and still breathing, then God is not finished with you yet.

All our days are NUMBERED, like the proverbial hourglass over your head. Not to be blunt, but the cold hard facts mathematically mean, the sands of time on this planet are only DECREASING with every single day you are drawing breath.
Begin to appreciate each and every one.

I have deep respect for those in the medical field who are genuinely there to provide a high standard of care and compassion, however they are still human. They can, and do, make mistakes. Lots of them. In fact the THIRD biggest killer in the US is medical malpractice. Nearly a quarter of a million people DIE just from medical errors. That is around 200 000 innocent men, women and children E-V-E-R-Y year.

This would happen to Chanel when she was just over 12 months old.
The medical team at a local private hospital dismissed my intuition and motherly instincts as "first time mum syndrome" (aka over-reacting), when her father and I turned up distressed to Emergency late one night. She was very unsettled yet seemed fine and happy on the outside. The problem

was, she wasn't feeding at all, nor was she taking any water and it was in the middle of a hot summer.

According to one of the paediatricians, had I taken her home that evening, things could have played out very differently and ended in her little kidneys failing. It was later discovered she had a serious, yet hidden infection that was only found via a blood test. That blood test only happened because I stood my ground, and firmly told the medical staff that I was not leaving the hospital that night until the medical team investigated further. Needless to say they apologised profusely when the test results came back.
She stayed in the hospital for 3 days and made a full recovery.

They can mis-diagnose. They can shrug off, or completely miss infections. They can miss tumours. They can make mistakes in the operating theatre. They can prescribe the wrong medications or too many medications. There is FAR too much emphasis, in my opinion, in the God-like status that many place on their physicians and specialists. It's almost as if someone wears a white coat, then they are God and everything that comes out of their mouths is gospel.
No.

You know your body better than anyone else.

There is not just one way of doing things, and if you are in the throes of what feels like an insurmountable health crisis and encounter this, if your gut instinct makes you feel as though things do not sit quite right, then listen to your intuition and request more time, more tests, go elsewhere, seek and research other options.
PERIOD.

My personal experience around the immunotherapy conversation was probably one of THE most eye-opening moments of my life. To feel as though I was in a production line and being stamped and pushed through an overburdened and failing system just to tick boxes.
I would often look around the waiting rooms in the Oncology Out-Patients Ward and literally feel the despair, the *"this is it for me"* energy, just sitting

and waiting for their number to be called, literally accepting whatever is, without QUESTIONING anything. Sad. The system is just so broken.

Yes of course, you must take the hand you have been dealt and make the most of it. This can and will, usually involve an influx of immediate emotions and tasks, however it is also HOW you handle the situation moving forward. We can either be a VICTIM of circumstance or we can have VICTORY over it.

Most people do not, or will not, participate in their own rescue. BOOM.

How many people do you know that will happily regurgitate their experiences over and over and over but not actually DO anything to fix it, or at least try to find a solution or new perspective? Most of us have probably been there at some point in our lives. I know I have. Life lessons. And usually, we all know at least one person who actively participates, directly or indirectly, in their own DRAMA.

You may think you don't have a choice or weren't given a choice right now. And that may be true. There are many situations where you are not responsible for the hand being dealt. Nevertheless, from this moment on, we CAN choose how we FEEL, how we RESPOND, what we do next, how we interact with those who may be involved and how we view ourselves and the situation at hand moving forward.

"...focusing on what you cannot do instead of what you can do creates a picture of yourself and the existing narrative that is limited and incomplete..."

MIRACLE INSPIRATION: Take your POWER back.
Never let anyone decide for you.
Victim mode will keep you on the same road.
No matter what it is you are facing.
Change your perspective.
If nothing changes - nothing changes.

Always remember - you are special.

You are unique.

You are one of a kind.

There is no one in the world like YOU.

So walk with certainty.

Walk with purpose.

BE in the driver's seat.

Victim or Victor?

You decide.

••

> "I am proud that I defy your categories. I am proud that I don't fit easily into any box. I am proud of all the things I am and all the things I can be. Question yourself every time you think you only see one thing in me." ~ David Levithan

••

Chapter 6

SPEAK UP ....AND
ASK QUESTIONS

....

"At the centre of your being you have the
answer; you know who you are, and you know
what you want." ~ Lao Tzu

....

There is an old saying: Knowledge is power. True. But without the APPLICATION of knowledge, it is just thoughts. Only when knowledge is APPLIED does it begin to CHANGE the results. You can wish all you want, however without INSPIRED action it is just a wish.

Too often in life and especially in the medical realm, we ACCEPT what is, without questioning "Is this it? Or "Is there more?" "and "Are there other options?"

The answer is usually YES!! Yet we have become so bound and conditioned to the fact that what is said is FINAL. I keep reminding those impacted by cancer especially, that it is not the end of the road or the end of the world. It is actually showing people WHERE they need to HEAL or what needs addressing or changing the most. Start by finding the ROOT CAUSE of the cancer. And I mean physically, metaphysically, food, lifestyle, thoughts, stress, mindset, emotional pain and past trauma. Because the answer, and the healing, will be in there somewhere.

Every day there are thousands of people around the world taking matters into their own hands, questioning their diagnosis, researching other therapies, or applying and adding other modalities to their existing treatment. And HEALING! The medical establishment is just ONE way. And in my personal opinion, it is failing miserably. So many people are falling through the cracks of a tired, outdated and very fixed, pharma-funded and strategic structure.

Remember, this is impacting YOUR body, YOUR health, YOUR life.
You have a say! In fact, you have THE say. Yes of course talk things out with the appropriate professionals, friends and family, but ultimately the bottom line lies with YOU. This applies to everything in life. Stop giving your power away. This was probably one of the hardest lessons for me to learn.

Fear – usually of the unknown – will cripple all of us at some point, to either shrink back, stop dead in our tracks, not make a decision, or have others make the decision for us, falling backwards into familiar territory or allowing others to dominate or control outcomes in our lives. People-pleasing is another big one a.k.a weak boundaries. I'm sure you've been there before? Not wanting to rock the boat by voicing your concern, opinion, or feelings, so you shut your mouth and stay quiet.

Teach yourself to SPEAK UP.
Be brave.
Stand up for yourself.
Ask the right questions.
Or demand the right answers.

Just because someone gives their opinion or point of view does not mean you have to ACCEPT it. When you accept, consciously or unconsciously, to what is being put forward, it is accepting an ENERGETIC agreement. You are automatically complying by default. Think of it like a business transaction. Are you happy with the terms and conditions? Are you satisfied that this is the best offer being presented? For me, it was a resounding HELL NO!

If those around you do not see your value and worth or respect your decisions, or ability to question, then they are not your people. Find a new tribe who are aligned with your vision, who will support you, cheer you on, listen to you and walk the path alongside you.

Going through this while covid was playing out on the world stage was also another layer to navigate. Thankfully and by God's divine grace and protection, I managed to avoid the dramas and restrictions with my frequent hospital and specialist appointments.

I did, however, observe many people become numb, sheepish and silenced through mandated masks and almost communist directives. I could often feel the fear and the collective energy of people with so much to say yet feeling forced to comply against their free will.
Akin to a global throat chakra blockage.
Censorship and restrictions on a deeply personal and planetary level.

Yet behind closed doors, and in the comfort and protection of their own homes and environments, or with people they could trust, their voices mostly told a different story. Words of distress and stress. Sadness, grief, sorrow, angst and frustration at what was taking place in the world. Their inability to feel as though they could control anything. Feelings of helplessness and uncertainty. High levels of silencing and the editing of words and emotions.

We have predominantly been conditioned in life to be quiet. Be polite. Not rock the boat. Not be too confronting or conflicting. Stick with the narrative. Don't think for yourself. Just follow. And definitely don't verbalise what you are thinking or feeling!

Throughout life, I am sure you felt compelled within specific situations to express a valid and important point of view, yet were silenced and instructed NOT to speak up as it may cause conflict or an imbalanced outcome. Even if it was the TRUTH. Yet internally, this simply created further frustration and chaos as things continued to fester within you.

Or perhaps at times, you felt stifled or suppressed, yet deep down you had an overriding inner knowing that to vent or voice your opinion, or truth, would have been the preferred and better option in hindsight. You literally suck it up, believing you have done the right thing, or you feel it simply won't matter in the long run. Yet deep down, either whilst the scenario is playing out (or afterwards), feelings of agitation and possibly resentfulness set in, as a result of ALLOWING others to take the reins.

That, my dear beautiful readers, is usually a MASSIVE sign that you have ignored your intuition and your own personal boundaries. You are not a doormat for others to continually wipe their feet on as they help themselves to your time, energy and resources. In all honesty, sometimes the best thing you can do is literally lose your shit to ultimately maintain your own inner peace. Those who disrespect your boundaries never respected you in the first place.
Truth.

Sometimes we all have to draw the proverbial line in the sand with certain individuals. It may not solve things in the moment, however your voice would be heard and those repressed feelings would have their time and place to be acknowledged. Speaking UP and speaking OUT in life usually requires BRAVERY and courage as well as going against the grain of deep societal conditioning. Women especially.
And yes, that means it might be rather daunting and scary.
Granted, if those words are harmful, abusive or projecting your own inner shit, that is a different scenario. I am highlighting expressing yourself with conviction and integrity, together with authenticity and truth. Not raging out of control like a bull at a gate.

It took a significant length of time when I was younger to find the courage to speak up. And not everyone will be a fan when you do. Not everyone will like your opinion. Not everyone will like your choices. Not everyone will accept your stance on a situation. And that is ok. It is not about winning universal approval or appeasing everyone. It is about YOU. And no, not in an egoic, selfish way.

It is about you finding your CORE truth in situations, and with people, and voicing it in a way that is diplomatic yet also from your SOUL. Your soul wants to be HEARD. And sometimes in certain situations that can be blunt and brutal. Yet still very valid. Never apologise for how you FEEL. Just be MINDFUL of placing yourself in a situation where you must apologise later for how you REACTED in the heat of the moment. Big difference.

Along this journey I know not everyone initially understood my methods or my choices, but I sure as hell didn't mince my words, or have any grey areas in my communication, or in how I wanted things to roll. And as with most major crises in life, there were people who had their own opinions on how I should have handled things, or protocols I should have incorporated. Yet I constantly reminded myself, that is ok. Others are ALLOWED to have their own opinions. Most of the time it was emanating from a genuine place of caring, truly wanting to help, or feeling like they were contributing in some way.
And they were. All of them. To some degree. In their own special way.

Remember - Your journey is no one else's but YOURS.

Therefore, in reality, no one can ever truly understand what YOU are going through, because the greater majority have never experienced YOUR story. Not even close. They've only experienced THEIRS. Therefore, whilst there may be similarities, they mostly witness or respond to your story from the level of their own life experiences, that then ultimately influences or determines their own personal view of the actual situation at hand. It's almost illusional.

How can someone truly understand another soul, if their own reality, upbringing, life experience and perception of a challenge has been so vastly different to yours? It's like looking at the same thing through two completely different lenses.

At the end of the day, no matter what is going on around you, no matter other's opinions - BELIEVE in where you are headed so strongly that nothing fractures your vision or your faith.

"…your path is for you alone to walk…"

MIRACLE INSPIRATION: Speak up and speak out.
Voice how you feel in an unapologetic yet non-threatening way.
If you can't voice it – then write it.
Sometimes you might just have to write it - and then BURN it.
Hashtag #Just saying!

Be ok with others not understanding you.
Be ok triggering others with your words if those words are your authentic truth.
Be ok with having the courage to question.
Be ok to keep asking until you find your answers or your core truth in situations and with people.
This is about YOU.
And how your words, feelings and opinions are RECEIVED is about them.

· ·

"A single event can awaken within us a stranger totally unknown to us." ~ Antoine de Saint-Exupery

· ·

Chapter 7

HEALTHY MINDSET –
MASTERING YOUR MIND

You are what you SAY you are.
And you are what you THINK you are.

....

"Be strong-minded and always believe that
the impossible is possible." –Selena

....

The battle, and the VICTORY, starts and ends here.
Always.
No matter what you are dealing with in life.

Whatever program your mind is currently running internally and externally
on the health diagnosis, the relationship, the job, the money, the whatever -
is what you will ATTRACT - and will usually be HOW you handle LIFE.
This, for most people, is usually on complete autopilot.

Throughout our time on earth, we have two dominant programs and
frequencies at play - positive and negative. Where your current dominant
thought process goes and FLOWS, is how you will handle your daily
existence and usually life's challenges. By mastering your mind through
acknowledging, removing, and replacing outdated and often embedded

beliefs, patterns, programs and behaviours, you will begin to see life FLOW in a different, more POSITIVE energetic direction.

Imagine your mind is a mobile tower, (because it is!), beaming out frequencies on whatever you are thinking about - 24/7. The more energy and EMOTION and thought behind a thing, a person, a situation, **positive or negative,** if it is in alignment with your existing subconscious programming, it will eventually show up in your life, in one form or another.

For example, anything in life that you like, and these things come to you easily, is because you have a dominant thought program to support and attract and anchor that. A car space is the classic example. Holding a predominant, confident and EXPECTANT thought, that every time you go to the shops you will easily find a car space, will predominantly bring about that result and it will predominantly BE your experience.

However, the contrast is, whatever you are working hard and pushing and pushing to achieve, anything you are struggling with or are having major RESISTANCE in bringing to reality, may stem from a dominant subconscious program sabotaging your desired outcome. It's not a match because there is a 'frequency displacement consciousness' around it. Therefore, anything you are trying to accomplish, whether it is health or love or a work goal, your subconscious program must be in ALIGNMENT to support the desired conclusion before it will come into your existence.

The exception to this rule is if something or someone is NOT for you, for your highest good, or for your highest purpose, then God/Source/Spirit will shut that door, bolt it, blow it up and send the ashes out to sea. Likewise, if it is meant for you, then it will align or possibly RE-ALIGN and materialise into your life at the perfect time. What is for you, cannot go past you. What isn't will be removed.

If we simplify it and stay focused on the basics of mindset, the positive news is, right now at this very moment, you can begin to reprogram and change old patterns. Every moment, every thought – you have a CHOICE. Whatever seems to be elusive to you, whatever you feel you can't have or feels out of reach, the universe isn't holding it back, it's usually your own invisible subconscious patterns. Once you begin to truly understand this, you will begin to realise that **most** challenges that you are facing in life, it's not God or the Universe causing the issue, it's YOU. It simply may have taken hours, days, weeks, months or years to manifest into your reality.

Now you have your first inclination and understanding of HOW to begin to change your current challenge, and potentially your life, because now you know what the predominant underlying issue really is.
This is the most important part. You can change the programming. You can rewrite your underlying, subconscious beliefs.

Once you learn how to flex this mindset muscle and begin to merge your conscious desires and wishes with the new subconscious programming, your mind will automatically start to take you in that direction. Now both are running congruently together.

For me personally, after the initial shock and adjustment to what was showing up in my reality, I was able to mentally switch into my predominant program on divine faith, wellness, and healing. Because this is a strong mindset muscle for me. It has always come naturally for me to BE this way, LIVE this way, and inspire and motivate others to do the same. So regardless of whether it was a test or a manifestation from the past, or both, I knew deep in my soul I would be ok – eventually. Leaning into faith and trust in the Almighty Creator, I knew that I would HEAL. Because this is the dominant program in my mind.
BE-ING HEALTHY.

I just had to flex my mindset muscle and keep it strong.
On point.
Every day.
Showing up and doing the work.
Internally and externally.
And fuel it.

> You can be a victim of cancer, or a survivor of cancer. It's a mindset. –Dave Pelzer

Your mind is the trojan horse. It can easily bring you down or lift you up. We always have a choice. Even in the depths of what feels like total disaster. It is stronger and more powerful than you can ever possibly imagine. The famous saying, "whether you think you can or think you can't, you are right" is so true.

I chose every day to say, *"I can. I will. And I am – HEALING."*

You are more resilient than you know. You are a warrior, with everything within you to overcome your battles, along with a bucketload of inner strength just waiting to burst forth.
But it all starts in the MIND.
When you feel you are at breaking point and cannot go on, remember, you are in fact using about 40% of your inner mental strength. Therefore if you truly knew the level of determination and infinite power you have deep inside the core of your being, it would literally AMAZE you!

Anchor these words deep in your soul. Allow them to set off a spark that ignites into a flame and finally into a blazing fire of self-assuredness that YOU CAN DO THIS, and you will get through this!
Whatever "this" is.

Nothing will show you just how much you are capable of, until you face a major health crisis, life adversity, loss of a loved one, job, partner, finances or death and especially when it happens without warning. It is only in these moments of major personal crisis and emotional conflict that you truly understand the depth of this strength and your capacity to handle what is in front of you.

For me, I continued making it a priority to strengthen my mindset. To address any old fear based and limiting programming around healing running on loop.
I made the intention, and the COMMITMENT, to accomplishing my goal. Intention is not wishing and hoping. It is the pure determination to CREATE the desired outcome. It is the dominant use of your WILL. And we all have FREE will. So, again, in each moment, YOU get to CHOOSE FREELY where your intention and will goes.

I listened to and ABSORBED countless YouTube videos on mindset, staying focused, not quitting, strengthening my faith, moving forward, and moving through adversity. There are literally thousands of free videos that require zero monetary investment, that will lift, inspire, encourage, and motivate you – no matter what you are facing – or feeling, at this moment.

I did whatever I could to reprogram and FEED my mind with words of strength, resilience, grit, determination, faith and an unquestionable deep seeded belief that God had my back (and always will), and is always in control. ALWAYS. No matter what.
I have not once since then, made it through a single day without listening to at least one podcast, one video, or reading one post that does not reinforce all these empowering qualities deep into my cellular being.

According to experts, the average person thinks approximately 6000 thoughts a day. Some say a great deal more. The tragic part is, statistics also show that around 80% of those thoughts will be negative! Do yourself a favour, check yourself regularly throughout the day and COMMIT to them predominently being positive. Where your MIND goes is where your LIFE goes.

Make it non-negotiable.

Comparable to an exercise routine. You can get fit, lose weight or build muscle, however if you stop, your body will eventually LOSE what you have worked so hard to achieve. It must become a lifestyle choice and an INVESTMENT in yourself to keep showing up to do the work and maintain the results. The same principle applies to our mental health. Over time, bad habits and old thought patterns can creep back in. We either get lazy. Or complacent. Or comfortable. Or all three.
It has become almost a mantra for me to feed my mind like I feed my body. I had made it a disciplined routine to live an active lifestyle, showing up to the gym for decades to strengthen my body, training to feel good for maximum health benefits, yet I did not have a regular routine for my MIND. Crazy.

For years, I fed it all kinds of daily rubbish, reflecting now on what can only be described as a wasteland of negative news, pointless tv shows, and regurgitating work dramas and relationship issues, as well as consistently listening to and absorbing other people's daily frustrations, and family obligations. My mindset was subconsciously anchored (predominantly) by inherited and learned childhood beliefs, patterns, and programs, essentially growing up in an environment of dysfunction and drama – in all of its forms.

The defining moment when the lightbulb finally switched on, was a mixed bag of emotions including anger, frustration and regret, felt mostly from the precious time I wasted in that headspace. However, in these major ah-ha moments, kicking yourself while you are down doesn't help. It's not about blaming or punishing, it is about GROWTH. And that growth took place when I was willing to finally face my inner shit once and for all. I took a good, hard look in the mirror at the outdated and pre-programmed loop I had been playing in the background on repeat.

So true to the Law of Attraction, what I was listening to, thinking about, adding energy to, and subconsciously running deep in my mind, I was AMPLIFYING and primarily inviting into my reality. Of course, we are all human, and we cannot exist only in the realm of constant positivity. We need both the shadow side and light side for polarity, context and balance. This is life. If we don't experience the contrast, we won't know what we truly DO want to have or create.

Life is the total sum of what you consistently THINK about and SPEAK about, who you surround yourself with, as well as what you are watching, reading and listening to, that ultimately CREATES and DOMINATES, what shows up in your vortex as your daily reality. Furthermore, add into the mix the intensity and energetic charge from any highly emotional scenarios you are actively investing into. These key areas are regularly highlighted on an energetic checklist for me and I perform a stocktake frequently to ensure my vortex is predominantly positive.

Likewise, vibrations, in the form of arguments, relationship issues or breakdowns, repetitive negative self-talk, job and general life stresses and more, are sent out like magnetic shockwaves into the universe, therefore, essentially and unknowingly, placing a cosmic order for more of the same. As such, and true to the laws of attraction and manifestation, you are silently and unconsciously attracting additional negativity from a lower vibrational state, that in the long term, can and WILL manifest in the body also.

The mind manifests.
The body listens.
And so it is.
In my case, literally.

Imagine your brain is a computer being downloaded with software and the latest updates. What are you unknowingly and intentionally installing or uploading? What old or outdated programs are you continuing to refresh or download again onto your computer every day? Most of us, metaphorically, are either consciously or indirectly receiving and reading what I refer to as "brain spam". A daily inbox of recycled deleted emails with subject lines from past relationships, news headlines, childhood trauma, job losses, petty grievances, family breakdowns and more, sometimes repeating from years gone by, over and over and over.

Additionally, almost all of our social media, television shows and general day-to-day entertainment channels are DESIGNED to keep you in a perpetual state of feeling inadequate or not enough, distracted or needing more of something, instant gratification, comparison syndrome or feeding fears, insecurities and addictions.

Personally, I ceased watching mainstream television more than 15 years ago and it was hands down THE best decision I have ever made for my mental health. I no longer listen to constant news headlines led and fed, mostly by fear, death, destruction and sadness. I no longer participate in reality shows designed to mindlessly distract, influence or promote people's five minutes of fame. Whilst I remain AWARE of current events, any form of media I give my time, energy and attention to is my CHOICE. So, I choose wisely. My choices in movies or social activities are predominently happy, positive, funny and uplifting - entertainment that leaves me laughing and FEELING good!

Because I want more of that.

Needless to say, you and I are here, along with the entire planet in these 3D human meat-suits, and at some stage will FAIL. At times spectacularly. That's life. As long as you are failing forward, not falling backwards – every experience in some capacity is GROWTH. There will be days, sometimes more than not, that you will likely fall into the funk and spiral headfirst to the bottom of the mountain, and that is OK too. I have been there more times than I can count. In fact I'm sure I set up base camp there and bunkered down for lengthy periods at different times in my life. Old programming will rear its ugly head, repeating on autopilot like an old movie reel.
Simply acknowledge it.
Feel into it.
Then ask yourself - where this thought is coming from? Is this mine or have I taken it on from someone else or somewhere else?
And most importantly - is this true for me at this moment?

These thoughts might be silent fears, words or actions that were said and done to you. Perhaps you failed at the same thing previously or experienced major setbacks and gave up. Maybe they are deep subconscious programs that you INHERITED or BELIEVED as a child, words that were spoken OVER you that have been stored deeply in your psyche that once perhaps protected you but are now keeping you STUCK and small.
And sometimes, we just feel plain old TIRED.
Over it.
Couldn't be bothered.
It's all too hard.
And that is perfectly OK too.

Once the root cause is determined, it is then finding a way that works for YOU to release it, heal it and move on. In some instances, the simple act of self-realisation and that magical ah-ha moment may often be enough.
For more traumatic situations, you may need to find a specific healer, alternative therapist or integrative practitioner to assist you.
For me, Emotion Code and Body Code are very effective modalities in shifting and clearing trapped emotions as well as being fast and painless

in releasing the root cause. I have used a beautiful practitioner in the UK (link below) on and off for many years on both myself and Chanel, however practitioners are based worldwide, depending on your location. With similarities to reiki, sessions do not need to be in person and can be conducted remotely anywhere in the world.

Home (lightofnirvana.com)

It is staying in victim mode or defeated mode and keeping the negative, lower vibrational energy swirling around you that is the most destructive and dangerous to your mindset. Nothing will bring you down faster than reliving, recycling and rehashing old damaging junk. This is where anxiety and depression and regressing into the proverbial black hole can cause us to shrink and sink into what I like to refer to as Shrek's muddy swamp - The Forest of Illusion.

It is ok to have a bad day, it is ok to cry, it is ok to rant, it is ok to get frustrated, go silent, feel overwhelmed and all of the things, but it is how READILY you are willing to process those setbacks or emotions to dust yourself off and get back up again. Do not bypass this step. Do not try to suppress the emotions or put a band-aid over the top, ignore it and pretend to be all positivity, rainbows, unicorns and love and light.
Essentially this is extremely damaging to your SOUL and also a form of bypassing, both mentally, spiritually and physically.

There is not one single person on this planet that hasn't had a bad day, or two or ten, or hundreds. And there will be more. We all experience these. We are all light and dark. And it's only through facing the shadow side that we can release the emotions, heal, move forward and grow.

Just don't let the shadows and emotional mud pull you so far down that you end up staying there.

At times for me, life seems to mimic certain days in the gym, where I am just not up for it. I honestly wish I had an avatar that could do it for me because even I get lazy or don't want to deal with things. True story! I simply want to follow the same old routine. Because I know it. It's easy. As with life, sometimes I don't want to do the hard stuff or attempt the new. And some days I follow that comfortable and well-travelled path or make excuses from a place of procrastination, self-sabotage or disinterest. It is the same with challenges in life. Sometimes it takes time, discipline, dedication, and a WILLINGNESS to push through those moments where you simply feel you cannot handle anymore of life's weight on your shoulders - but you CAN.

....

If you can build a muscle, you can build a mindset. —Jay Shet

....

I remember my beautiful mother towards the beginning, sending me a little hand-written letter and as I opened it up there was a smaller, tightly folded printed piece of paper.

It was a long list of **I AM** statements. Two of THE most powerful words ever spoken, for what follows them are energetic statements to God/Source/Spirit/Divine Creator/the Universe, but more importantly, you are RE-AFFIRMING what you have spoken out loud to YOURSELF and your own MIND.

Most people will say these two words on autopilot without even realising what follows . The Universe hears and delivers more of whatever it is that's being constantly thought about and spoken about.

I AM ALIVE!
I AM BLESSED.
I AM GRATEFUL.
I AM HEALTHY.
I AM HEALED.
I AM WHOLE.
I AM PROSPEROUS.
I AM SUCCESSFUL.
I AM VICTORIOUS.
I AM TALENTED.
I AM CREATIVE.

I AM WISE.
I AM MAGNIFICENT.
I AM COMPLETE.
I AM FIT.
I AM IN SHAPE.
I AM ENERGETIC.
I AM HAPPY.
I AM POSITIVE.
I AM PASSIONATE.
I AM STRONG.
I AM CONFIDENT.
I AM SECURE.
I AM BEAUTIFUL.
I AM ATTRACTIVE.
I AM VALUABLE.
I AM LOVED.
I AM LOVABLE.
I AM FREE.
I AM REDEEMED.
I AM FORGIVEN.
I AM ANOINTED.
I AM ACCEPTED.
I AM APPROVED.
I AM PREPARED.
I AM QUALIFIED.
I AM MOTIVATED.
I AM FOCUSED.
I AM DISCIPLINED.
I AM DETERMINED.
I AM PATIENT.
I AM KIND.
I AM COMPASSIONATE.
I AM GENEROUS.
I AM EXCELLENT.
I AM WELL EQUIPPED.
I AM EMPOWERED.

I AM WELL ABLE.
I AM A SOVEREIGN BEING.
I AM SURROUNDED BY GOD'S FAVOUR.
I AM A CHILD OF THE MOST-HIGH GOD.

I kept it the entire time and on some of my worst days, I would repeat these statements out loud in the mornings when I first woke up. Mostly though, I would read them and repeat them in my mind.

> "....if you realized just how powerful your thoughts are and how your thoughts create your reality, you would never think a negative thought again..."

MIRACLE INSPIRATION: What are your mental programs? Are you consciously and actively creating your life from a place of AWARENESS or are you unconsciously drifting along playing old programs on repeat like re-runs of a tv show?

Look at your current challenge or adversity that you are facing right now. Whatever it is that you are struggling with, the struggle is not always because God/Universe won't provide a positive answer for you, it's usually because the struggle is an internal job, and subconsciously you are trying to overcome previous beliefs that are preventing you from achieving your desired result.

Remember, It's virtually impossible to think positively and speak negatively and expect a favourable result. And vice versa. If one of these isn't in alignment with the other then that area of your life will most likely feel as though you are pushing the proverbial uphill.

If it is grief and loss, I send you big hugs and love.

Set up a DAILY ritual for your mind, no matter how small, to EXERCISE it and FEED it with proper "nutrition", not junk or mindless garbage merely distracting you and keeping you stuck, spinning the wheels and in an unknowing state of influence and self-sabotage. Remember most people are thinking negatively a high proportion of the time. Imagine what would happen to your mindset, your disposition and your LIFE, if you listened to, and spoke positively for the same amount of time?

Furthermore, just as RECOVERY is required for the body, use your time WISELY at night if possible, to implement evening meditations that can be played whilst you sleep to anchor in your daily work.

These action steps were fundamental in my healing process.

● ●

Changing your mindset may change the situation. –Lisa Rusczyk

● ●

TEAMWORK MAKES
THE DREAM WORK

Support Crew - whose got your back

•••

"In the end, though, maybe we must all give up trying to pay back the people in this world who sustain our lives. In the end, maybe it's wiser to surrender before the miraculous scope of human generosity and to just keep saying thank you, forever and sincerely, for as long as we have voices."
— Elizabeth Gilbert

•••

BACK YOURSELF FIRST.

Always.

No matter what.

You are your biggest investment in life.

Then make it a priority to surround yourself with your own water-tight cheer squad. You know the ones. Those special people who genuinely love you, can and will, offer support and unbiased advice or words of wisdom.

A team of amazing humans who are reliable, honest, and literally will stand rock solid by your side no matter what.

For me, I would personally rather just one of these beautiful souls beside me than a whole auditorium of shallow, wishy-washy, in and out, flaky fake friends and associates who are there on the side lines and jump in just for the drama or good bits but disappear or bail when the shit really hits.

With me, you are either all in or all out. I don't do grey or middle areas. Small investments will get you small returns. I simply look at it from the timeless perspective of, you get you what you give. And when I am committed to something or someone, I am ALL in.

Looking back though, there have been multiple times throughout my life where I have walked in my own strength and solitude, and have been ok with that, but honestly, when life throws you a curveball, and I mean the mother of all curve balls, or takes a hefty swing that sits you firmly on your backside, you need to have an amazing, supportive, tight team of people in and around your presence.

You just do.

Energy is contagious. It TRANSFERS. Remember, you are a mirror and the total sum of all the people, places, things, situations, emotions, what you watch, what you read and what you listen to. So be especially discerning in the CHOICE of people around you, no matter who they are. They will make or break your life in so many ways.

Unfortunately, at certain times in life, that may mean that family (or particular family members), may take a back seat, or you simply shorten your times with them. The same applies to your friends. There will be some that you may need to park to the side, spend shorter times with or just take a break from completely. Remember, it's not personal, it's just ENERGY. It is the fine art of BALANCED energy exchange.

You will know by the way they leave you FEELING.

I can be unapologetically short and sweet with my company at times, yet this is by no means a definitive reflection of how important that particular person may be in my life. If my energy is low, I KNOW that I won't be able to expend, or expand, my energy positively in their presence. Likewise, if the person's energy is rather superficial, time-wasting or low investment, I may come across as short, sharp, and quick to wrap up my valuable time with them. I am simply observing my own mood and "energy charge" and being mindful and selective on who and where I spend it. More so now than ever before.

A classic example would be the battery in your mobile phone. If the battery is very low or drained, most will tend to keep their conversations short and to the point because they know the phone could go flat at any time. The same applies to every conversation, every person, every situation. They are either draining your battery or charging it.

The nuts and bolts of it all, is when in the company of others, especially your circle, how they feel is how YOU will usually feel – especially by the end of the conversation. And how you FEEL is especially important to how FAST you HEAL, whether that is through a personal crisis or actual physical healing. I have been so incredibly blessed and fortunate to have had some amazing souls step in or step up on this journey. Spirit has truly surrounded me with a select team of the finest people along the way.

After the initial diagnosis was given and the dust had settled, Jay and Bianca sent out (unbeknown to me) an email to my old work crew explaining my situation and asking them if they would like to help support me, in this critical time of genuine need.

Words cannot express the deep gratitude and shock that I felt when I heard virtually everyone had put their hands up to contribute.
And they continued to do this without question, every single week for three solid months!

This ONE gesture, this beautiful act of kindness, support and outpouring of love changed everything for me. Their selfless generosity fueled my will to keep up the fight, allowed me to focus on the vast number of initial appointments, scans and tests, but more importantly, it allowed me to focus on my daughter and my healing, without additional stress around expenses, income and providing continued financial stability for Chanel.

Interestingly, God will, on occasions, use those who may NOT be your biggest fan yet they will feel strangely compelled to help or reach out in some way, shape or form. God can use anybody at any time to move you along your path, assist you or supply what you need at the time, so always be OPEN to receive from surprising or unusual sources.

To this day I truly struggle to talk about that defining moment without the tears accompanying it. Their contributions, along with unbelievable personal and company support from Jay and Bianca, literally paid for my week of radiation through my private oncologist and then some. To these beautiful humans it was simply helping a colleague in a time of true need, however the ripple effect penetrated far deeper than just the financial aspect. In my heart, I felt the deep level of love and respect they had for me as a crew member, mentor, and friend, but mostly for Chanel, juggling the day-to-day basics for her, in between everything else as a solo parent. Who does that? What company does that? No one I know. That is for sure.

There are simply no words to ever describe the level of gratitude and appreciation I had (and have) for each and every one of those amazing human beings.

What you give, GROWS.

As such, I sent forth my gratitude prayers every week to God and the angels and asked for each person to be blessed and recompensed for their kindness and generosity. My prayers were answered quickly as I watched and listened to events and company records being smashed out of the ballpark. Personal records were broken, and overall, everyone who had selflessly committed to supporting me, received their own unique blessings and rewards.

"You get what you give."

Bottom line, when people have your back and show up, not only will YOU benefit from their genuine loyalty and support, but THEY will generally feel good and most often be REWARDED and blessed in unexpected ways too. The beautiful part about giving, is the more you give the more you receive. It can be time, money, support, small gestures of kindness, compliments and more. Abundance and blessings are not just about financial rewards. There are so many ways that you can be blessed!

Being vulnerable and saying, *"I can't do this on my own"*, or *"I need help"* or *"I don't know what to do at this moment"*, is not a sign of weakness. In fact, it is a true sign of humility and STRENGTH. Society, and especially social media, has taught us to soldier on, do it all, look amazing, filter everything, show the best not the worst, spruke the wins not the losses, continuously live in a state of false and unattainable perfection at all times, pretend everything is fine or hide behind various daily disguises.

It is admirable to have resilience and confidence, although when the external mask is hiding deep pain, loneliness, physical limitations, a need for validation, approval from others, uncertainty, or deep insecurity from living in a completely edited and filtered world, this can manifest in our ENERGY FIELD, our soul, our psyche and ultimately into our physical body.

Protect your heart around strangers. However, remain open with your vulnerability with those who confess to genuinely love you, have your back, front, and sides, and want to see you HAPPY. Your tribe is your tribe. Treasure them with all your heart and reciprocate regularly, when and how you can.

There is freedom and liberation when you take off the mask. Even Superman and Wonder Woman were regular human beings by day with pressures, jobs and commitments underneath their superpowers and external bravado. It's ok to not be ok - and ASK for help and support. True strength lies in vulnerability and openness.

When we share our rawness - and REALNESS - warts and all, our heart expands, our energy is open and we make room to ALLOW those who love us and want to help us - IN.

> "Always remember people who have helped you along the way, and don't forget to lift someone up."— Roy T. Bennett

MIRACLE INSPIRATION: There will be many people undoubtedly in life who will try to knock you down.

Just don't be one of those people to YOURSELF.

When the chips are down, instead of isolating, tuning out and thinking you must do everything yourself or you can't possibly impose on others (a past habit of mine), rally your nearest and dearest around you like a fortress that cannot be penetrated.

Allow them to fuel what may be nothing more than a tiny, flickering flame left within you. Allow them to support you, protect you and to help you, so you have more strength to move through the turbulent times - no matter what.

· ·

"Today I am grateful for all the people who are loving and kind to me…. For they are a simply a reflection of the love and kindness within me…" Unknown

· ·

Chapter 9

WORDS MATTER
- as you speak so shall you sow

"Keep your thoughts positive, because your thoughts become your words. Keep your words positive, because your words become your habits. Keep your habits positive, because your habits become your values. Keep your values positive, because your values become your destiny." – Gandhi

This is quite possibly the second most important piece of the puzzle to master behind mindset. In the beginning was the word - and everything begins with a word. This signifies the importance of the words you speak.

The old saying - *"where attention goes, energy flows"* - is true. You are literally in a state of manifestation every single moment of the day. Mostly through the words you SPEAK.
Whatever you are predominantly speaking is usually what you are predominantly MANIFESTING.

However, did you know, other people can send YOU positive or negative energy simply with their words?

All words are verbal SPELL-INGS.

One single word can have a permanent impact.

It can uplift or completely destroy.

The tongue is powerful.

The words you speak can be as sweet as candy or pure poison.

And if there is intensity behind those words (and emotions), they can infiltrate your energy field.

Positively or negatively.

For example, if those words are of love, support, kindness and success being spoken about you or over you, then that beautiful energy will emanate all around you. You will FEEL good. In the midst of our own challenging situations, or whilst assisting someone else in the midst of a crisis, the more thoughtful and non-judgmental our words are, not only brings help and HEALING to ourselves but also to others.

Equally, if it is words of negativity, jealousy, anger, bitterness, hatred or contempt, then these destructive words will also impact you, sticking like mud to your mind and aura, lowering your vibration and leaving you feeling defeated, drained, sad or resentful.

The words we use, and the WAY we deliver them are essentially verbal affirmations of our innermost thoughts. Use them wisely. Use them as a tool to help instead of to hurt. To HEAL instead of affirming illness.

All words consist of sounds, and every sound has a VIBRATION. Put simply, every single word has its own vibration and these vibrations create the world around you.

On the opposite spectrum are the vibrations of ANGER, such as "I HATE XYZ!" In fits of rage or heated arguments for example, intense feelings like anger can send powerful shock waves into another's energy field. And unless you know how to protect your own energy, if this person walks away and continues to think, SPEAK and feel that anger towards you, you will energetically FEEL it too. Of course, the person speaking it out and sending it out is also energetically affected. This can often mirror back and manifest in some form on them as well. However consistent energy attacks, over time, can fracture and weaken the other person's auric field. Some might say it is a form of "cursing" others or a form of psychic attacks.

You may be familiar with those moments when you have had an intense argument with your partner, or a work colleague or a random stranger on the road or at the shops. You feel those less than comfortable vibes not only spilling out of you but also being projected outward like invisible daggers from the other person. Most likely your inner GPS (guidance protection system) is picking up the negative frequencies and wants you to exit the room, road, or immediate environment ASAP!

Words are incredibly POWERFUL. What is constantly repeated, either OVER you by others, such as family, friends, work colleagues, even strangers, but also what YOU think and say about yourself, will eventually show up, not only reflected in your physical environment, but literally physically in your body.

Every word you speak is prophesying your future.

Imagine for a day, every single positive word spoken over you and to you, and about yourself, is written on a post-it note and stuck to your body, and all you did throughout your day was collect positive words and attach them to your body. At the end of the day when you pulled them off and read them, how do you think you would FEEL? Hopefully positive and uplifted, loved and happy!

Now imagine you collected all the negative words spoken over you, and to you, and to yourself. As you read each one, how do you think those words will impact your mental attitude and how you FEEL about yourself? Would there be more negative than positive? This is a very profound way to understand the immense potency words have on us.

Which vibration are you PREDOMINANTLY living in?

As I reflect on past experiences I now understand that the YEARS of mental stress, anguish, conflict, worry, court battles, arguments, mind games, and plain old fuckery from my ex, were a leading contributor to the brain cancer diagnosis.

Back story: Five years earlier, I was unfortunately in the middle of high tension and distress associated with the same person and ended up in hospital. I thought at the time it was nothing more than a small but cautionary procedure to have a tiny freckle removed from the middle of my back that had been there since I was a child.

I clearly remember arriving home from a work trip, feeling incredibly stressed from the consistent, relentless drama and catching it in the bathroom mirror the following morning. This tiny little dot had suddenly changed from its normal slightly tan colour to a dark, almost midnight black. My thoughts at the time were a little perplexing as this small freckle had been with me for a good 45+ years and was probably one of only a couple on my entire body with not so much as a change in size or colour – EVER. Naturally, that little intuitive gut feeling said, *"You better get that checked. That's not normal."*

My GP took a biopsy the following week and at the time assured me it was nothing to worry about. However, when the test results returned, it warranted having it removed. No big deal I thought. On a scale of one to ten, one being nothing and ten being extremely serious, it came back as a one. To err on the side of caution, my GP decided it should be removed.

However, rather than the procedure being relatively short and painless and simply carried out at my local medical practice, it morphed into a referral to a local skin specialist. This led to my admission into a local private hospital for a day operation, culminating with the surgeon removing five of my main lymph glands from the middle of my back, through to my feet and under the left armpit. I was absolutely devastated when I came to. I was informed prior to theatre there was a slight chance of extracting maybe one or two small ones attached to the freckle only.

Now five is not a huge number, in fact it is minute given the human body has between 500-600 lymph glands, but these were main pathways from under the arm, the middle of my back and connecting all the way to my feet. Essentially an important part of the major highway around my body.

Imagine blocking five main highways around the area where you live. Imagine the peak flow of regular traffic on those highways every day. When an accident occurs to close parts of the roads affected, the traffic generally deviates to side streets, the nearest off ramps or detours. I'm sure you've been caught at some point in your life to appreciate how slow and frustrating and CONGESTED it becomes?

Now imagine that a vast majority of the cars stuck in the traffic jam decide to bypass the accident by taking the nearest side street or off ramp. Where once the major highways would usually facilitate moving volumes of cars and trucks smoothly, the off ramps suddenly become the alternative route. These then become jammed and SWELL, unable to handle the sudden volume of vehicles simultaneously.

This is essentially how the body initially responds to major lymph glands being extracted. By permanently removing main roads around the body, it results in the redirection of lymphatic fluid, and forces the body to re-route it to the smaller glands that, in turn, are unable to cope with the immediate volume and pressure.

At the time, I felt coerced by well-meaning family and friends to have it taken care of, given Chanel was still very little. The next morning I woke up extremely sore and swollen. Within 24 hours, my left arm had blown up to twice its size with post-op lymphedema, as my body struggled with the sudden change, ultimately taking 5 days for my body to recalibrate and adjust. Truthfully, my lymphatics have not functioned efficiently since, regardless of diet, exercise and water intake. I honestly reflect on this moment and question, did that operation open my body up for the cells to spread?

I guess I may never know the definitive answer there. However, during routine blood tests, nurses would often comment on the many stories of patients in similar situations. Of course, reflecting on timelines and scenarios, I feel it probably played a contributing part.

That, coupled with being raised on a farm some 45 years earlier, surrounded by fertilisers, weed killers and other agricultural concoctions. Exposure to these chemicals have been known to cause abnormalities and weaknesses in the structure of DNA. Unfortunately, in the 70's, there were virtually zero safety measures or precautions taken because there was virtually zero education and information on the long term effects. So many probable factors and possibilities. In many ways, it was essentially the perfect storm brewing from multiple angles.

What was certain though, was the destructive energy and the volatile environment I was immersed in at the time of my marriage breakdown, including the many years following. Strong words and vibrations of hatred, frustration, anger, blame, worry, deep sadness, constant conflict and despair. There was no OFF button. It was equivalent to being under attack from an invisible barrage of knives and feeling as though I was at war and in the battle trenches 24/7. Completely relentless and extremely damaging on so many levels.

> "Words kill, words give life: they're either poison or fruit – YOU choose..." SOLOMON

If there was reprieve, it was short lived. At best, there were small snippets of peace where the situation became slightly bearable. Then the cycle would commence ALL OVER AGAIN. I vividly recall at times feeling so defeated, so drained, so mentally exhausted after YEARS of this repetitive toxic pattern, that I kept praying to God to please make it stop.

The game changer came the moment I realised and understood that I had the CHOICE and the POWER with my words, to either REACT or RESPOND.

Reacting is what most of us will do in the heat of the moment. We tend to fire off at the person or situation, then vent about it again to friends, repeat, and recycle it over and over at least a few more times, either in our own minds or with other people in our closest circle, before we make up, cool off, it's dealt with, or we simply walk away.

All the while, in this state, we are unknowingly ADDING negatively charged fuel to the energetic fire. The more we regurgitate it, the more energy we are continuing to FEED it. The more you feed it, the more it GROWS. Every single word is released out of our mouths and into our energetic field, then directed at the situation or person causing the conflict.

When you speak negatively you are breathing those words into LIFE.

And vice versa.
If it's a long-held battle, on-going conflict, or daily sore point, then this impacts on our day, our interactions, and our mental and physical body. This begins showing up as S-T-R-E-S-S!
Believe me when I say, you can stress yourself out, not only from the triggering situation, but as a result of the words you speak and the conversations you feed into.

I like to refer to it these days as emotional spew. It's not very pleasant to imagine, however, in these moments, we are either verbally throwing up over other people, or unfortunately, often internally spewing negativity over ourselves. Is it any wonder then, that stress can literally make us sick?

The more neutral and positive way to vent, express our emotions or just plain old communicate, especially in times of high conflict, is to RESPOND as calmly and as maturely and as balanced as possible. In high conflict that is easier said than done. I know.

The words we use when we emanate from this place of neutrality and non-attachment are far less destructive energetically. Usually, when we respond, even if it isn't always in our favour, or to our liking, our vibrational field is less fractured, and we are more likely to bounce back or move on more quickly. Our energy field will usually clear and recalibrate a lot faster too. We literally "shake it off."

Mastering our words (and emotions) is a true form of self-mastery.

Some might call my choices excessive, however I frequently burn sage in the evenings to cleanse and clear negatively charged energy that I may have collected from conversations and interactions with others in my day-to-day routine.

I may be predominantly operating from a higher state of awareness and choosing my words and conversations wisely, yet that doesn't mean everyone else around me is too.

Yes, I even clear my phone. Extreme you say? Don't dismiss it. Isn't it one of our main forms of communication throughout any given day? Take a moment to think back on the conversations and the WORDS you have spoken today for example, and the words you have RECEIVED, along with the energy from those conversations THROUGH it. And in these modern tech times, our phones are also mini-computers with access to the internet, emails and all types of social media. Hundreds, if not thousands of words, both written and spoken right there! Begin to think about the ENERGY attached to all of that. On some level you are ABSORBING it. Even if it is incremental. At the end of the day, it is simply another form of energy exchange and as such, needs to be cleared and cleansed regularly too.

Many experts agree that regularly detoxing and decluttering the mind is important to overall health, however, I believe that if we did a daily detox of the words we CHOOSE and USE, our health would automatically improve too. In the same way you take out household garbage, it's equally important to metaphorically take out the daily trash from your mouth, and your mind, that is mentally draining your energy or stressing you out.

One of the most negative actions in the height of a crisis or adversity, is to catastrophize the situation out loud and then continue to repeat it in your mind. Especially if the situation being spoken about or thought about has not physically happened. If you are verbalising the worst possible outcomes, these negative thought patterns and pessimistic self-talk begin playing on a loop inside your mind and ultimately begin GENERATING more of the same. I have been guilty of this on many occasions at various stages in my life. Mostly it is projected outward to those who will listen, impacting their energy and absolutely impacting YOU and manifesting again and again.

Naturally, this is extremely challenging to do when the situation is entirely out of your hands or your reputation and name is being slandered against or attacked, and you are being deliberately provoked to elicit a REACTION.

Outside of ensuring your own personal safety, you have every right to be defensive and protect yourself. My advice however, is instead of engaging in hostile situations or challenging scenarios that may generate and ESCALATE out of nowhere, take a few deep breaths and disengage, both verbally and physically if you can. You will thank yourself and your mental and emotional health later.

In these instances especially, begin thinking and speaking to yourself P-O-S-I-T-I-V-E-L-Y. You may not be able to change what is in front of you but you CAN change what's INSIDE of you .
All change begins from WITHIN.

Think of it like a set of scales.
What ratio of positive vs negative do you feel your scales would show?
If it's under 50% positive, then Houston we have a serious problem!
Instead of trying to immediately attain 70% or 80% or 90% - start with manageable ways to increase your positive self-talk and personal energy in increments.

Small, yet powerful changes, include ditching and switching the negative news and latest updates, to listening to, or reading, at least 20 mins of upbeat, motivational or positive affirmations, music, podcasts, or whatever you are drawn to. Do it DAILY. In the car, on your walk, in the background while making breakfast or preparing dinner in the kitchen, playing through headphones while you are working on your computer. You get the idea. You know your routine, your day, your availability to make it happen. If time is very restricted, then break it down into 2 x 10 min sessions in your day.

Whatever works for you.
Then build on that.
And build on that again.
And again.

The more your mind ABSORBS encouragement, positivity, motivation, and a CAN-do attitude, the more inspired, resilient and in control of your circumstances, yourself, and your TONGUE, you will become.

Think, and speak predominantly what you WANT – not what you don't want.

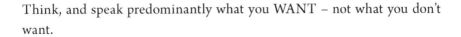

> "What you radiate outward in your thoughts, feelings, mental pictures and words, you attract into your life." – Catherine Ponder

Be aware of the ENERGY when around others, having general conversations, or those times you are brought into someone else's drama or conflict.

Be aware of how you felt before and after.

Does your vibration increase or decrease around those you engage with and are the words and conversations more positive or negative?

If you feel guided, write it down, making note of any emotions that may be bothering you in your specific situation.

Ask yourself are they MINE?

Or THEIRS?

Or is it COLLECTIVE energy?

Release it if it's not yours. You would be surprised how much collective dirt and negative junk can accumulate in your own energy field by simply interacting with others on any given day.

And in a health-related situation like mine, NEVER allow others to speak ill-health or a medical diagnosis OVER you. Most people automatically OWN their illnesses and ailments and announce them like a badge of honour every time someone asks what is wrong without even consciously realising it. Their words are pre-programmed, with little to no attention or thought given to the POWER they are unknowingly releasing out of their mouths.

Examples - I am a diabetic. I am getting fat. I am suffering from arthritis. I have cancer.

Every single time you talk about your health problems and it is repeatedly ATTACHED to you, you are reaffirming it, reinforcing it and so it is. This equally applies to others talking about your health problems, such as your doctor, your friends, your family, your work colleagues and even writing it on social media.

I'm not saying these issues don't exist, instead begin by re-phrasing HOW you word it.

The doctor said it is diabetes. The diabetes is causing a few issues.
It is time to lose weight. I am prioritising my health.
The arthritis is playing up and a little painful/sore/uncomfortable.
The oncologist said it is cancer. The cancer is in the brain/bowels/lungs etc.

You can reword anything that you are trying to communicate.

You are still saying it, but you aren't OWNING it or ATTACHING it to YOU. They are neutral statements but not personalised, therefore the energy doesn't continue to compound back OVER you every time it is spoken. Begin correcting your family and friends each time they speak something negative or not in alignment with your desired health goals, because at the end of the day, it is REPETITION.

How many times have you or others said, "I am SICK and TIRED of/ that... ..... (fill in the blank)? When you SAY and HEAR something long enough, the subconscious mind BELIEVES it, confirms it and continues to give you more of the same. Repeat. Repeat. Repeat.

I did not and do not take OWNERSHIP of any sickness, dis-ease, or diagnosis and I rebuked, cancelled and deleted any and all contracts binding me to any diagnosis and I certainly did not and do not allow others to speak ill-health over me.
Ever.
Only healing and perfect health.
Always.

MIRACLE INSPIRATION: Become DEDICATED, RUTHLESS and RELENTLESS to editing your words and your story. Because your words will eventually create your reality.

Edit or Delete anything or anyone that disempowers you or your goal. And keep pulling yourself up - not beating yourself up - when you think or speak negatively too. Because it's going to happen. You are human.

Every time you are feeling stressed out, maxxed out or under fire or challenged, decide *"Is this thought, statement, conversation, person or situation, useful/beneficial/positive"* to my desired feeling or outcome?"

No? Then start there. Either change the thought pattern, change the words, change the circumstances or change your perspective to something more positive. If that seems too radical to begin with, then at least change the verbal dialogue enough so that your mind SHIFTS towards the end goal.

Then prepare to watch your situation and life begin to change.

....

"Words are singularly the most powerful force available to humanity. We can choose to use this force constructively with words of encouragement, or destructively using words of despair. Words have energy and power with the ability to help, to heal, to hinder, to hurt, to harm, to humiliate and to humble..."
Yehuda Berg

....

ENERGY HEALING - in order to HEAL we must be willing to FEEL – and release trapped emotions - "feelings buried alive never die"

> "If you want to find the secrets of the universe, think in terms of energy, frequency and vibration." Nikola Tesla

The discomforts we carry in life become energy blockages in the body. In turn, these energy blockages affect our mental and emotional state along with our physical body.

Where in your body do you feel you have been storing old wounds from past hurts, grievances, deep losses, broken relationships, family conflict or generational trauma?

Let's take a few common examples. These are very generalised and not specific. Pain, discomfort, tightness in the neck, shoulders or lower back is generally related to feeling unsupported, financial worries, feeling burdened emotionally, as though you have the "weight" of the world on your shoulders, carrying stressful responsibilities, or not willing to be flexible.

Suffering from skin flare-ups or breakouts such as acne, eczema or rashes? Perhaps ask yourself, who or what is agitating or irritating you? What have you been suppressing? Are there inner conflicts resurfacing?

Gut issues, such as IBS can relate to not wanting to digest or accept life. Inflammation in the joints particularly hips and knees can mean irritation or anger at a situation or someone, lack of purpose in life or a fear of, or stubbornness to move forward.

Headaches and migraines relate to mild to intense inner pressure, fear, anxiety getting the best of you, inability to face issues or resolve emotional upsets, disliking feeling "pushed" along by people or circumstances, or pushing for control or wanting to control.

What about excess weight? The term overweight is generally an abandonment issue stemming from a person or people of significance such as a parent. It can also represent boredom or living a dissatisfied life. The waist signifies the need for protection, and feelings being unexpressed or "stuffed" inside. Thighs is usually resentment from father issues, insecurity, rejection, seeking love and fulfilment.

These are just a few very small, (and very broad) examples of how trapped emotions store themselves in parts, functions or organs in the body and manifest into either minor, short-term issues – or into serious, long term health problems.

Every single area of your body, when out of alignment, or in pain, or suffering a dis-ease or illness of some description, has a metaphysical root cause and meaning.

EVERY.
SINGLE.
ONE.

Do not dismiss this unbelievably valuable piece of the healing puzzle! No matter whether it's purely emotional right now or whether it's physical or both.

This one hidden and often unknown nugget can be the catalyst for true healing – on all levels. We can seek advice and treatments from the doctors, the specialists and other gurus who may prescribe the pills and potions, and of course, these may help you, however it is YOU and your body that is doing the actual healing. Not them.

Energy healing is not woo-woo. In fact, the traction it is now gaining across many fields is a positive sign. Reiki for example, is an immensely powerful and recognised modality and just one form of energy healing.

Reiki means "universal life force" or "energy in motion". Medical establishments such as integrative wellness centres and some hospitals offer reiki as part of their patient services. Imagine the difference in well-being and HEALING if this was available to patients in all hospitals across the world.

Both Chanel and I have undertaken many sessions with a beautiful friend and Reiki Master over the past few years. My intuition automatically signals when either of us are out of balance and our energy centres (chakras) need clearing, healing and rebalancing. If you are under stress, feeling tired, emotional, or have been through, or are in the midst of a personal crisis, I highly recommend locating a reiki practitioner in your area for a session. If that's simply not possible, reiki can be channelled and received remotely anywhere in the world.

Remember, everything is energy. We are energy. In fact, we are approximately 37-70 trillion cells of pure divine energy and therefore we all have access to our own body's ability to heal itself. It is when these cells begin to build up life's garbage or emotional waste that our physical bodies begin to get sick or manifest more serious health conditions.

. . . .

"Nothing can change unless our body and mind are playing on the same team."— Poppy Jamie

. . . .

Let me give you an example for cancer. Now this is general. Cancers in different parts of the body also have slightly different metaphysical meanings. There are unfortunately too many to list here and not all cancers form tumours, which are mostly the storage and collection point for all the unhealed emotions in the body. Any wonder when they are cut out, the toxins contained in those tumours are released back into the bloodstream and form elsewhere or they reappear years later if the emotional healing has not taken place.

In its most generalised form however, it means - SELF-DESTRUCTION. It is the SOUL crying out for help internally because it needs LOVE.
Woah.

(GENERAL) CANCER: feelings of limitation, anger, fear, feeling out of control, carrying burdens from the past. Suppressed long term feelings of not being good enough, shrinking back from others or situations, literally attacking yourself from the inside. Feelings of guilt, grief and uncertainty all "eating away" at your body. Feeling on guard, never able to relax or let go and often pushing oneself to do/be more than one can handle. Trying to please others.

This description hit me so deeply as I came to terms with the accuracy, and accepted, that this in part, manifested from YEARS of constant high-level MENTAL anxiety and emotional stress, being ABSORBED and STORED from court battles, multiple betrayals, the divorce itself, consistent aggressive, bullying behaviour, threats, abusive messages, phone calls, manipulation around our daughter and the subtle yet relentless gaslighting.

The brain is the most important and most protected organ in the body. This is why God intentionally surrounded it by bone, and a liquid cushioned barrier (blood brain barrier), that protects and prevents damage under a physical attack or in an accident. The human body is truly magnificent and complex. Yet, none of this external armour will save you when the brain is being attacked from the INSIDE. Mentally, emotionally and relentlessly. Those impenetrable physical shields are useless when the MIND is ambushed, invaded, bombed and under seige internally.

Metaphysically, the brain represents LIFE. The brain is also the command centre, the control tower, and directs EVERYTHING our bodies do. The brain also directs our life, and for many it will predominantly be on autopilot and a total sum of everything experienced in a person's existence upto that point.

Therefore, unless we acknowledge, forgive, delete, release, reprogram, heal and grow, our brain is simply STORING and recycling these experiences and emotions, positive and negative, in some form in its hard drive.

Therefore, when the hard drive is full and a sudden shock or tragedy hits, beyond what the brain is capable of understanding or rationalising, or able to find a solution for, it will feel as though you have lost all CONTROL, are completely overwhelmed and in an elevated and constant state of CHAOS as there is no way out and no foreseeable solution. This is *generally* how illnesses and diseases in the brain manifest from a metaphysical level. In children, I feel that it may be passed on through fractured DNA from trauma experienced by the mother, or generations prior, or the family home environment, surroundings and dynamics.

••

"Brain problems affect susceptible and receptive people who are experiencing external situations that cause great confusion." Emotions and Body

••

Consequently, these situations were simultaneously playing out whilst under pressure to maintain high level work commitments, juggling to wear multiple hats, and raising Chanel who was around two years of age at the time. It became a calculated and very strategic operation and usually the other person is completely blindsided at the depths to which an ex-spouse, partner or loved one can go. At times, as I previously mentioned, it was literally WAR. And as you know, war doesn't just end when the day is over, you are tired and have had enough.

There is zero time out.

There is no stop button to catch your breath.

There is no time to regroup or take a break.

There is however, fighting, bloodshed, feeling as though you are in the battle trenches 24/7, extreme pressure under very unstable conditions, minimal or broken sleep, continuously operating on high alert and high adrenaline, not knowing what will happen next or if it will ever come to an end.

I had to educate myself on how to RESPOND not react and completely detach to snuff out the "fuel", being conflict and drama that narcissistic behaviour thrives on. My life was a constant juggling act to provide a stable loving home environment for Chanel in amongst the turmoil. I won't lie. At times it became almost unbearable, yet I had to keep standing. Living through this experience has given me such a deep understanding of others in similar situations, who truthfully end up in the foetal position in the corner, feeling as though they are living in some kind of hell on earth with their soul simultaneously being syphoned out of them.

Because essentially, they are.

Our bodies are, of course, very adept at handling stress, coded into our genetic makeup via cortisol release in times of fight or flight. However, over time, elevated levels of EXTREME stress has been linked to numerous health complications, weak, failing or malfunctioning immune systems, and of course the long term manifestation in the body of more serious diseases, like c-a-n-c-e-r.

In a nutshell, stress can, or possibly could be, physically making you SICK.

Stress takes its toll emotionally but also exacerbates virtually any health issue you can think of.
Studies have proven that stress on the body increases your risk of asthma, depression, weight problems, heart disease, Alzheimer's, diabetes, gastrointestinal issues and more. It truly is dis-EASE in your body. In fact, doctors say that high level emotional stress can also be a trigger for serious cardiac problems such as inflammation to the heart muscle, changing the way your blood clots and potentially triggering the big ones - heart attacks and strokes. Stress has also been shown to accelerate ageing by between nine and seventeen years!

When we take the stress out of our lives, or at the very least REDUCE or take steps to minimise our daily exposure to it, our bodies can RELAX and begin to HEAL.

Looking back at my dysfunctional, damaging and difficult childhood, I now understand why I had chronic asthma. Studies have shown that parental stress affected the rates of young children being born with or developing asthma in their early years. Children with "stressed out" parents, or those holding unresolved grief, also had a significantly higher risk of developing asthma.

Metaphysically, asthma is related to feelings of trying too hard to please others (nothing was ever good enough for my father who was stressed out most of the time), grief (my brother's sudden deaths), not standing up for oneself or being able or allowed to express one's feelings, hopelessness, "what's the point?", feeling defeated or pushing to one's limits, often striving for perfection.

ALL.
OF.
THAT.
Tick. Tick. And tick.

Asthmatic children may often feel weak, disempowered, and anxious, especially if their parents are high achievers or forceful and in turn can feel stuck, hurt or even caged in, almost suffocating and unable to "breathe", especially in controlling environments, such as the one I grew up in. My childhood was all these things, and more on than off.

As a child at times, it was so volatile I wished I wasn't there. That I was dead. Because then I would have peace. Then I wouldn't have to listen to the arguing, rage, uncertainty of the mood my father was in, the constant walking on eggshells, as at any given moment it could spin on a dime and go from tolerable to nightmare.

And in the true sense of manifestation, as asthmatics are susceptible to, I "swallowed my tongue" on a few occasions. I vividly remember one night feeling as though I was suffocating, literally stopped breathing and passed out. When I came to, my father was holding me by my feet upside down, outside on our front patio on the farm in the cold night air, belting the middle of my back trying to get me to breathe with my mother beside him, crying out to God to save me. And in that moment, outside of missing my mother, I remember praying that God would have just taken me instead.

Another catalyst moment ingrained in my memory forever. Only now, it's simply telling a story. Thankfully, with many sessions of body code and emotion code over the past few years especially, I have released the energetic and emotional charge around these experiences and cleared a lot of family dysfunction and ancestral trauma passed down through previous generations. I forgave my father in my twenties when I consciously understood he was simply regurgitating the anger and the hatred and hurt from his own horrid childhood with a controlling alcoholic and abusive father as his example.

Children learn what they live.

True healing can only take place when we forgive. Forgive the person. Forgive ourselves. Completely letting go of all resentment and anger gives our soul freedom too. It doesn't mean we forget. Instead, it no longer AFFECTS us in any way, shape or form. We simply no longer care, and the energetic charge no longer exists.

Hands down though, I feel UNHEALED generational and childhood trauma, (showing up as trapped emotions), is one of THE biggest causes of sickness, family distortion and dysfunction, child abuse, domestic violence, drug and alcohol addictions and more.

We store these experiences so deeply within our psyche, it spills out into our relationships, our careers, how we handle challenges and stresses, and later as adults, infiltrating and affecting our own sense of self-worth, self-love and self-respect. As we grow into adults we often repeat and ATTRACT that same energy or similar patterns in partners or friends or in our work environments because it is STORED in our energy field, in our cells and our DNA.

"Everything is energy. All energy has a frequency, a vibration. White light is made up of the rainbow of colours, red with the lowest frequency and violet with the highest. Humans are made of matter, which is made of energy.

If we take the most powerful microscopes and zoom in on any cell in the body, we go past the cells, DNA, base molecules, atoms, and electrons all the way down to quanta of energy and a lot of space. What is mind-blowing at this quantum level is that the act of observing these subatomic particles changes how they behave. It is as though they are aware of us and make decisions."
— Sandie Gascon

Think back for a moment to any conversation where you may have said to close friends, or to their children or family members, *"You are just like your mother/father/uncle/grandmother etc?"*
We are literally ENCODED from conception. Not only in mannerisms or looks but also GENERATIONAL trauma that is entombed in the DNA. This can be passed from one family lineage to the next. Not only through the DNA from your ancestors and parents, but right down to your parents home environment, the words they spoke, the foods your mother ate as it formed your body, the bad times, the joyful times, absolutely everything is being absorbed and STORED, then passed onto us as babies.

Suffering from chronic asthma as a young child, I was medicated up to my eyeballs at times and the side effects weren't much fun either. I gained the usual steroid weight, my face became puffy, I felt tired and fatigued A LOT and subsequently felt extremely unhappy because I wasn't "normal" like the other kids. I was absent frequently from school and sat out sports regularly. As my body's capabilities changed, so did my ability to participate in outdoor sports and general activities like other children, and as such began to feel excluded physically and emotionally. As I grew into a teenager, my capacity to participate in school activities or with friends continued to decrease. These emotions manifested into feeling almost unloved and worthless as body image is strongly highlighted in the teen years. It became a vicious cycle. I hated my body for being uncooperative, physically tired, and unable to do what I wanted it to do.

Bucketloads of suppressed and stored emotions right there.

Energetically, it therefore makes sense that many kids with childhood asthma go on to completely "grow" out of it when they reach their adult years. Most likely, as in my instance, they leave the environment that was literally suffocating them and create their own homes and spaces without the pressure or emotional stress of the parents or triggers around them.

The truth is, if you are currently facing a health crisis or suffering from long term unhealed emotional or physical health issues, then perhaps it is time to address the ROOT cause. Maybe it is suppressed emotions from childhood or maybe it is a result of ALLOWING your body to be a daily dumping ground from your own thinking and other people's unresolved, unhealed energies as you have grown into adulthood.

Is it a garbage tip of stored emotions from these past experiences? Regardless of whether it was a word, an emotion, a specific time or event from your early years, or a combination of life experiences as you have grown older, the body is LISTENING to everything you (and others) SPEAK, THINK and FEEL - over you, around you and about you.

• •

"So, as we get older, there's this cemented mud that gets stuck along the walls of our interior body and blocks our energy fields. When we decide to finally acknowledge that crusted traumatic event, we start to feel the discomfort as it's dislodging from our emotional body." — Lali A. Love

• •

Every single cell in our body holds a cellular memory. Bear in mind, we have, as mentioned earlier, between 37-70 trillion cells in our bodies and around 200 different types of cells, with a further 10-100 trillion microbial cells! ALL those cells are essentially mini receivers and transmitters!

You can now begin to understand HOW important our words, feelings and thoughts affect our physical health! And the words, feelings and thoughts of our parents, grandparents and ancestors! Our bodies are literally major power stations, sending OUT and drawing IN the frequency of our thoughts, feelings and words.

It is all layered and is so much more than just healthy food = healthy body. It is about HEALING the root cause from your CELLULAR memory so you can truly experience a healthy physical body, healthy relationships, healthy work environments and a healthy mindset.

••

"Emotions are energies showing up to guide us" — Jeanne McElvaney

••

Energy healing has undeniably been a game changer and lifesaver in my life. Years of reliving, releasing and of course, forgiving, changed me on a deep soul and cellular level. However this only took place in my late thirties and early forties and is still very much a project in motion. To be honest, I believe healing and self-mastery is a continual life-long project for anyone committed to doing the deep inner work.

Never is it so clearly visible in the world that many of us are carrying unresolved emotional scarring, and often (unknowingly) regurgitating these wounds over and over throughout each generation. No one is really addressing it, let alone acknowledging or healing it. If you experienced a beautiful childhood, then hand on heart - I hope that you feel truly blessed and grateful. As mentioned earlier, children usually learn what they live. I lived with criticism, anger, profound grief, fear, hard times and a lack consciousness. Yes, it taught me a great deal about life, but if we are to heal, and I mean TRULY heal, then we must heal ALL parts of ourselves, our family wounding and trauma bonds, as well as ancestral karma, curses, vows, contracts and covenants – our DNA carries EVERYTHING.

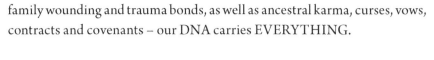

> "Today healing energy constantly flows through every organ, joint and cell in my body." - Louise Hay

In essence, energy healing is centred around removing the energetic blocks to the natural vibrational flow through your body, connecting the mental, physical and spiritual wellbeing. This in turn assists the body's natural healing ability and restores the balance between your mind, body and soul. Aligning the chakras and clearing the energy pathways, also called meridians, allows the chi to move freely and assist in this process. Every chakra is essentially associated with parts, functions and organs as are the main meridians flowing through the body. Therefore, many people swear by acupuncture, reiki and kinesiology, just to name a few.

Having been fascinated with this method for many years, I coincidentally completed an energy healing course in my early forties. Nothing is ever by chance, and I believe that small but powerful piece of the puzzle was strategically positioned into my timeline for this very moment.

There are so many other different forms of energy healing, such as crystal healing, QiGong, Pranic, EFT, and Quantum healing as well as bio-generators and RIFE machines. For me personally, emotion code and body code and using frequencies are a standout, as they isolate and remove the root cause, usually stuck emotions. The targeted frequencies associated with whatever you are wanting to heal or shift, then accelerate the body's ability to naturally restore itself.

Energy healing can improve health issues such as chronic pain, inflammation in the body, accelerate recovery from surgery or injuries, stress, anxiety, mood disorders, insomnia, cancer and more. Usually, the side benefits may also include feeling more balanced and at peace, feeling hopeful, more tolerant, and less likely to lash out in anger, accelerated spiritual growth and a greater sense of calm.

Go with your intuition. Perhaps you have already tried one, some or all of these. Perhaps you have tried none. Whatever is troubling you in this moment – ask yourself, if you were to consider one of these modalities, which one are you drawn to? Your higher self always knows the answer to what YOU need. I am simply opening your mind to other possibilities and alternative healing techniques.

··

"Energy healing is based on the supposition that illness results from disturbances in the body's energies and energy fields and can be addressed via interventions into those energies and energy fields." Jed Diamond

··

MIRACLE INSPIRATION: TAKE THE TRASH OUT – in every aspect of the word. All the stored, stuck and stagnant emotions you have carried since childhood, past experiences, as well generational junk, unless released in a healthy way, are contributing to your present experiences in current relationships, work environments and your own personal level of acceptance, self-respect and self-love.

And the catalyst – affecting your body through stress, pain, sickness or DIS-ease.

"...I am strong, I am grounded, and I am rooted in my being. I am connected to this Universe and to my body and I send it rays of healing white light ..."

Chapter 11

INTUITION MIXED WITH MODERN MEDICINE – TAPPING INTO, AND TRUSTING YOUR INTERNAL GPS

••

"Trusting your intuition means tuning in as deeply as you can to the energy you feel, following that energy moment to moment, trusting that it will lead you where you want to go and bring you everything you desire." -Shakti Gawain

••

An important note before you begin reading this chapter:

I have written a simple foundational outline of each individual modality used prior to the diagnosis, implemented throughout, or have continued using, alongside the supplements taken and the environment I created around me. Go with, and follow what resonates with YOU. I am simply conveying what worked for ME, what I was drawn to, compelled to try, implement, or use throughout. Of course, as the title suggests, these therapies and supplements were incorporated around the prescription medication.

To be completely transparent, I truthfully struggled taking the pharmaceuticals in the beginning, knowing what was in them, the initial reactions, and what they were essentially doing long term to my body. After a few months, I woke up one morning and thought to myself, *"I need to refocus here. My current thought process is not moving me towards my goal. It's in direct misalignment. I HATE taking these."*

Strong emotions and energy right there.

At that moment, I made a clear decision to shift my perspective again. I visualised the tablets becoming "multivitamins" and instead began charging them on my crystal mat. Don't laugh. Not long after that, the reactions settled down and I haven't had a reaction since. My mindset also fully shifted into believing they were exactly what my brain and body needed for healing. Perspective.

Did I have slip ups or deviation days? Of course! I still do. Regardless, I was driven, determined and focused to accomplish my goal. Remember, there was no Plan B. This goal was always about seeing it through until the end. VICTORY.
However that looked and however long that took .

I've found with basic human psychology most of us won't fully commit when it comes to tasks or goals that are far-reaching, challenging, seem insurmountable or just plain uncomfortable. Instead, many will attempt it half-heartedly or go all in at the beginning, like a new gym routine or diet, then falter or give up before the results even begin to show. The good old comfort zone. I have been guilty of falling into this on quite a few occasions. It's almost like a default button. Comfort zones keep us SAFE. We know what to expect, what we must do, what is usually coming or the end result. But there is no GROWTH, and usually little to no RESULTS in comfort zones!

When you are forced into an unknown realm, it is generally going to take a whole new level of DIS-comfort to achieve the goal.
I was always in the mindset of throwing everything at it right from the beginning. Therefore whatever difficulty, challenge, trauma or life event you

are facing right now, know that there will be rocky moments, uncomfortable moments, falling to your knee's moments, "I just can't do this anymore" moments, I'm tired/exhausted/just don't want to" moments. Have them. Feel them. But then get back up and get on with it anyway. You've come this far already. If you give up now then all of that previous expended energy, effort, time and progress is completely and utterly WASTED. If you give up or give in, by default, you LOSE.

Every time.
It's automatic.
Game over.

So, persevere! No matter what. One step at a time. Because it could be that very next step that changes everything and turns the situation around.

Know your end goal and focus on small, daily, doable actions that will move you towards your vision. In those early days, when the medical establishment deemed it completely unthinkable and impossible that I would survive, all I focused on was THAT DAY. And if that was too much, then I focused on the next hour.

If my mind began to wander off into possible future scenarios of what could or couldn't happen, I had to concentrate on pulling myself back to now, the PRESENT moment. Because the present moment is all that we have and the only moment that is certain.

And of course, one of the most important steps in my action plan was: TRUST GOD FIRST THEN FOLLOW MY INTUITION.

Even when my logical mind stepped in to give me it's two cents worth or whisper, *"Are you crazy?! This is either a really reckless decision or a very ballsy move."* The safety default button in my mind would remind me that what I was doing or about to do, was not medically common or mainstream or even possible.

Intuition is our own built in truth detector. In other words, what is true for me may not be true for you. Goosebumps when talking to others is full blown confirmation that my intuition is on the money. Goosebumps resonate with MY truth, but I am sure you have, at some point, had a gut feeling on something or someone and it turned out to be true.

Or, the opposite, you had that feeling and did not act on it and regretted it later? It might've been about a person you were wanting to have a relationship with, a job, co-worker, a re-route on the way home from work. That was your intuition. And you don't need to have others validate it because it resonates with YOU.

You just KNOW.

> Intuition is the ability to acquire knowledge without recourse to conscious reasoning. Different fields use the word "intuition" in very different ways, including but not limited to: direct access to unconscious knowledge; unconscious cognition; inner sensing; inner insight to unconscious pattern-recognition; and the ability to understand something instinctively, without any need for conscious reasoning. WIKIPEDIA

With all of that in mind, here are just a few of the healing modalities I trusted my intuition on, worked with, and believe will become the next big thing in combining western medicines, supplements and procedures with energy and frequency healing.

You are aware by now that everything has a specific vibration. Everything. There is even a specific vibration for the screen or book you are reading this on and your eyes that see it.

When it comes to our bodies, things that are generally the cause of sickness or ill-health, like viruses, pathogens, parasites and bacteria, also have their own vibration. It is common knowledge that scientists have used vibration and frequencies to disintegrate or implode these intruders in many studies. Depending on the type of cancer, it has many links to parasites, candida, mould in the body and viruses. Not pleasant to think about but all of us have varying levels of these in our bodies. A healthy body however controls the internal environment with precision.

In our day-to-day life, imagine an opera singer who can sing at the perfect resonant frequency of champagne glasses and shatter them whilst the tray remains intact. We know this can be done; therefore, the same principles apply to anything living in our bodies. Specific vibrations can break apart or destroy these pathogens without harming the organs, cells or membranes that surround them.

Nicola Tesla and Raymond Rife are probably the two most famous inventors of energy and frequency healing. For me, having studied energy healing and having had a fascination with it for many years, it was a no-brainer to incorporate these modalities into my own journey right from the very start.

SCALAR ENERGY: The essence of energy. The common denominator of the universe and of life is scalar energy. Scalar energy is recognised as a phase-conjugated, double helix waveform that supplies the template for repairing our DNA. It also disassembles toxins, like heavy metals, chemicals, viruses, bacteria, and foreign substances, by altering their molecular structure, making them inert and nonreactive. Scalar energy also stimulates stem cells for repair. In essence, scalar energy is the 'Holy Grail'.

In simplistic terms, think of scalar energy like charging each one of your body's cells, just like a phone charger. When the batteries in the structure of our cells are low or damaged, this is when dis-harmony and dis-ease can infiltrate. In other words, keeping our cells "charged" keeps them healthy, vibrating at a high frequency and in turn, keeps our bodies healthy and less at risk of illness.

PMEF – (pulsed electromagnetic field) therapy or pulse electromagnetic therapy is relatively new in Australia yet has been used in hospitals in Germany and Eastern Europe for over twenty years and is backed by thousands of clinical studies. It is FDA approved in the USA for brain cancer, bone fractures that won't heal, depression and incontinence.

Now you are familiar with the basics of energy and frequencies, your body also carries a charge or voltage. Chronic illness and injuries also have an associated LOW voltage. A PEMF machine is basically a charging system that increases efficiency similar to charging a battery. In essence, it is scalar energy healing but more specific. If the body's tissues are working more efficiently, then this allows it to regain its balance to promote homeostasis. PEMF does not heal, it only helps CREATE the energy to do so.

Around the halfway mark in my journey, I rented a PMEF body mat from a beautiful friend, laying down and resting on it 2-3 times a day for a solid 6 weeks. Some of the more advanced mats include full size earphones and light therapy to the brain and eyes as you lie there and relax for no more than 30 mins at a time, almost comparable to meditation. PMEF mats are programmed with specific frequencies for hundreds of health issues including cancer. The different frequencies assist the body in reducing pain, cellular detoxing, recharging, and regeneration.

More commonly, PMEF is used in the athletic arena for multiple purposes and benefits including faster healing time with injuries and operations.

Other benefits include increased circulation, increasing hydration, oxygenating your body to optimise nutrients, removing metabolic waste and toxins, neurological disorders, enhanced immunity in the body, repairing cartilage and tissue damage, just to name a few.

SOUND FREQUENCIES: Probably one of my main healing techniques. Simple, specific, readily available, and FREE. There are literally hundreds and hundreds of specific frequency music playlists that anyone can look up on YouTube for their own personal health issues.

Some of the most important ones that I personally used and listened to, mainly at night when I was sleeping to speed up the healing process were RIFE frequencies. My main playlist included sound frequencies for melanoma, cancer, blood diseases, viruses, detoxification (to assist the body in eliminating die off) and lymphatic drainage. **Spooky2Rife** and **DrVirtual7 Empower Dynamics** on YouTube allows you to easily search for what you specifically need help or healing with. Most of these are only 15-20 minutes so easily adaptable into anyone's daily routine.

Additionally throughout the day when home, I would play the Solfeggio frequencies listed below through YouTube on my TV and through my soundbar, so it filled my home with beautiful, calming, cleansing and healing energy.

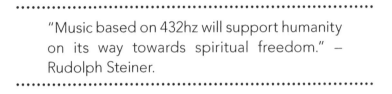

> "Music based on 432hz will support humanity on its way towards spiritual freedom." – Rudolph Steiner.

432Hz – NATURE'S HEALING FREQUENCY

This frequency helps in releasing stress and tension from the body and mind naturally, and unites the body and consciousness with nature. It helps release serotonin and endorphins, which in turn keeps blood pressure and the heart rate stable. 432Hz music also helps in releasing negative energy blockages and acts as a good sound healing tool to release toxins.

10 000 Hz / 728Hz – recommended as one of the best combinations of frequencies for most sicknesses when combined with 432Hz for sleep.
This combination is said to fully detox your glands, clearing and cleansing all seven chakras and eliminating diseases and viruses. 728Hz acts to remove unwanted microorganisms, improving and maintaining health and well-being.

7.83Hz Schumann Resonance - Heartbeat of the Earth

This frequency is resonant with the natural "heartbeat" of the earth which is why we feel so much happier and healthier when we are outside and CONNECTED to Mother Earth. Generally, we have greater mental clarity, tend to feel rejuvenated and relaxed when we spend time immersed in nature. As such, this frequency has been shown to improve our general health and wellness overall.

On the opposite end of the spectrum are our current daily regimes, spending lengthy periods indoors as well as being bombarded and surrounded by manmade EMF radiation. These routines are polluting our own biofield and causing a breakdown of communication between our cells in both human and animal bodies.

The Schumann Resonance is one of the most powerful frequencies in keeping our bodies in homeostasis, helping block EMF and 5G signals, reducing inflammation, increasing energy, reducing stress and anxiety, improving blood circulation, improving sleep and supporting recovery from intense workouts and physical activities.

> "Our entire biological system, the brain and the earth itself work on the same frequencies."
> Nicola Tesla

Additionally, your body is composed of approximately 70% water, and at the cellular level it comes in at nearly 90%. Therefore frequencies can positively affect cellular water clusters, and have the potential to aid in removing impurities from the cells in your body, to create a healthier cellular environment capable of fighting off sickness and disease.

Imagine if workspaces, hospitals, nursing homes and childcare facilities were filled with these frequencies in some form, and how this would positively impact these environments and the people in them?

RIFE FREQUENCIES:

In the early 1930s the brilliant scientist and medical researcher **Royal Raymond Rife** invented a unique microscope called the *Universal Microscope*. He was able to magnify live viruses thousands of times more than ever before, and he found that every virus had its own image, its own unique colour, and its own frequency. He noticed that when he broadcast a particular frequency at a particular virus, the inner body of the virus dissolved. The vibration then caused the cell wall to break open and explode the pathogen (any microorganism capable of producing disease) into the bloodstream.

These frequencies can specifically target virtually any health issue in the body. As I outlined above, I played Rife Frequencies for cancer and brain healing, along with lymphatic drainage and detoxification. I continue to play these often at night at bedtime. Similar to a meditation, I place my headphones in and let the frequencies run while I am sleeping.

I also want to clarify that you MUST listen to these DAILY and regularly, especially in the beginning. In other words, if you listen once and then stop, it's like going for a walk for one day but never going again or MAINTAINING it over time. There is virtually no illness or health issue or emotional challenge that you cannot find a frequency for!

An important side note on using these frequencies – DIE OFF. If you are treating yourself for specific health issues, there will be a natural detoxification process that happens within the body, as with a normal detox, so please ensure you are drinking plenty of alkaline water or lemon water to flush the metabolic waste out of the body.

To further explain the incredible benefits, the following information is extracted from Sound International Healing and can be found by following this link:

Benefits | RIFE FOR LIFE (soundresearchinternational.com)

SPECIFIC FREQUENCIES ARE USED FOR:

• **Destruction of Targeted Micro-Organisms (PANDEMICS)** - viruses, bacteria and parasite).

Specific frequencies are used to induce sympathetic resonance at the resonant frequency of the pathogen targeted. This literally explodes the target without harming healthy tissue that is not targeted. The insides of the targeted organism will become dysfunctional before the outer cellular wall ruptures.

Sometimes the nutrient pump will over pressurise the internal cavity, causing the outer cell wall to rupture first. This is all carried out without influencing non-targeted cells. The "mortal" oscillatory frequency rate targets and explodes viruses, bacteria, parasites, fungus, tumours, and calcium deposits, etc. By exposing disease-causing organisms to the proper frequencies, viruses and bacteria can be eliminated by the millions, leaving healthy tissue unharmed. Validated by decades of research, this technology can be used on pathogens and other metabolic deficiencies like:

* Influenzas & Infections: Viral & Bacteria *Arthritis * Fungus * Lyme Disease

* Allergies * Memory Loss * Herpes * Fibromyalgia * Chronic Fatigue * Parasites

* Candida * Migraines * Depression * Infections * Kidney & Liver Conditions, and most other conditions.

The list went on, as Rife watched under his microscope in the 1930's, making notes as to what pathogens were being affected by what frequency. These notes of Mr. Rife became the medical frequency manuals used today with the more advanced RIFE machines and are updated every year by ongoing research worldwide, helping to heal individuals who are guided to this amazing healing therapy.

· Turbo Charging the immune System.

Besides destroying micro-organisms directly, frequencies can be used to stimulate the immune system and thereby destroying micro-organisms with the support of the body's own defence mechanism, the immune system.

By using a frequency to target white blood cells, the body reacts with a homoeopathic response to produce an increase in white blood cells. This makes them a lot stronger to create a powerful immune boost. In addition, portions of the immune system, such as the thymus, can be targeted for stimulation to be much more active and dramatically increase their output.

· **Detoxing the Body by removing impurities** (pulverises toxic debris for elimination). Detoxifying frequencies shake loose the toxic debris from their storage locations and vibrate them into minute particles easily removed by the liver, kidneys, blood and lymph system.

(Please see Proper Cleansing Procedure)

· **Stimulating Regeneration by increasing cellular activity** (rebuilding through intentional sympathetic resonance).

Special regenerative frequencies are used to stimulate rapid growth five to ten times faster than normal, to repair broken bones, torn tissue and other damaged body parts that need repair.

· **Rejuvenating** (through stimulating body tissue, rebuilding DNA and reactivating cellular memory).

Internal body parts can each be stimulated with their own optimal natural resonant frequency to work, rebuild and repair faster. The internal mechanism frequencies are targeted to increase cellular metabolism to improve their function without causing cellular disintegration. It will regenerate cells, nerves, organs, bones, muscles, and tissue 5 to 10 times faster than normal – as well as building up the immune system, stimulating the thyroid, pancreas, the adrenals or other applicable organs.

· **Eliminating Addictions by rebalancing the body's energy fields** (add specific nutrition, emotional core release work and cleansing for comprehensive mind and body restoration).

Since the plasma tubes operate in the fifth dimensional energy domain, they are able to affect the body's energy fields directly. There are frequencies for alcoholism, tobacco addiction, cocaine, morphine and many others that are used to correct these energy field imbalances. The application is painless, unlike acupuncture, and the effect is immediate. There is even a frequency that increases the body's aura that can be seen in a kirelian photograph.

· **Balancing & Normalising Emotions** (through harmonic sympathetic resonance of targeted emotional frequencies).

There are healing frequencies for all aspects of the feeling body. Targeted emotions are called into harmonic realignment for their optimum placement to reconnect, balance and normalise emotional function. Eliminating worry, sadness, depression, emotional pain and trauma into a state of peace and tranquillity without any form of medications or harmful drugs. Transforming the vibration of fear and anxiety into a state of peace and relaxation within moments. There are frequencies that address and quickly correct the complete range of emotional imbalances.

· **Connecting Brain Synapses** (for emotional & neurological pathway healing).

This is especially important for neurological diseases when reconnecting is needed to restore bodily functions. This is carried out by using the specific frequencies that stimulate growth of the neurological connective tissues in the brain. Years of insomnia are often remedied in only a few applications.

· **Age Reversal** (a vibrational "fountain of youth" for mind, body & spirit). When body parts are rejuvenated and stimulated to function optimally, the mind is sharpened and the emotions balanced, and then age reversal is a reality."

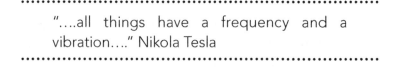

"….all things have a frequency and a vibration…." Nikola Tesla

AO FREQUENCY SCANNER: This amazing device is similar to a HEALY but on steroids and is based on the principals of RIFE. One of my gorgeous American friends introduced me to this incredible healing tool in the early days of the diagnosis. Its benefits impressed me so greatly I made the decision to invest in one for myself. AO stands for Alpha Omega scanner, and the following information has been extracted from the official website – "Every cell and organ in the body has its own distinctive vibrational frequency or oscillation. When these oscillations are disrupted, whether by injury, diet, stress or emotion, it results in a disruption of that biological function. Which when not addressed, can bring about fatigue, depression, illness, disease and even death. Over the past 20 years, more than 120,000 of these Vibrational Frequencies have been isolated, identified and catalogued. Knowing what the optimum oscillation or frequencies of these cells and organs are, can assist in determining the root cause of an individual's health status when these frequencies are compared to the individual scanned results.

1. Lists the detailed anatomy or components of each item that it scans
2. An elegant, yet simple method for measuring the health state of the entire body
3. Can project the health status out 3-5 years (unique amongst all non-invasive scanners)
4. a sophisticated electronic device that is capable of measuring these oscillations or frequencies utilising the AO Scan Bio-Transduring Headset
5. It presents detailed visual reports of the health status of the organs, systems, and tissue of the body, working similarly to other scanners in principles of measuring electromagnetic signals and the subtle bio-frequencies, but the brilliance here is quite literally in the details."

I ran different personalised frequency sets continuously, commencing around the two month mark and have continued using it on both myself and Chanel daily. The level of technology in these devices is mind-blowing. Everything from SEFI's – subtle energy frequency imprinters that include Quantum Reach, Quantum Frequency, Quantum Affirmations, Quantum Flowers, Quantum Chakras, Quantum Homeopathics and INNergy Homeo-Energetix.

I am able to run quick scans, EZ scans, Inner-voice, Vitals, Body Systems and Comprehensive Scans and reports on my body, Chanel, other people, as well as send frequencies for clearing and shielding to my home and car if I choose to.

Essentially, it is similar to having an owners manual for YOUR body.

Further information on this technology can be found by clicking my personal link below :

Home | Company Name (solexnation.com)

Initially, due to the nature of the diagnosis, popular alternative cancer treatment therapies such as hyperbaric oxygen therapy were blacklisted. It was devastating, as the protocols I had researched years earlier around treating cancer, were strongly rejected. The severity of the inflammation and clusters in the brain needed to be reduced and brought under control quickly, therefore anything impeding the medications crossing the blood brain barrier or potentially an accelerant for cell growth, could not be used or taken, or had to be halted immediately.

I struggled with these instructions in the beginning. Really struggled. I wasn't allowed antioxidants in ANY form. That meant zero greens powders, vitamin C, liposomal C, intravenous vitamin C, my B-EPICS that were full of mushroom extracts, pre/probiotics, superfoods, CBD oil, and many other usual protocols known to be the most well-known alternative therapies for cancer. I was devastated.

Again, I had to lean into trust and faith that I could navigate this obstacle and find other therapies instead.

And so began my research. This is something that comes naturally to me. Especially around health and wellness. I LOVE researching and educating myself on treatments, therapies, supplements and products that are new, cutting edge, or left field. I threw it all up to God and said, *"Please show me what I can do and where I can go."*

And again, through Divine intervention, and within 24 hours, I had found an amazing energy healing and alternative therapies centre literally 15 mins away from my home.

Three of the therapies available were given the green light from my oncologist immediately. Vie Light therapy, Red Light Therapy/Pod and Hydrogen therapy. To give you a quick snapshot - I laughed at my initial session of VieLight, as the "contraption" looks similar to something out of the old movie classic "Back to the Future"! It sits around your head like a halo and oxygen tubes are gently inserted up into the nasal cavity. The "halo" uses red light and pulse therapy while the oxygen into the nasal cavity works on increasing oxygen levels to the brain, without impeding or impacting any prescribed medications. In a nutshell - Vielight technology has the **most published research** in the field of safe, non-invasive brain **photobiomodulation technology**.

It sounds uncomfortable and very sci-fi, however it is quite the opposite. I would relax in the Scalar room on a large, comfortable recliner chair and continue with my work/phone calls or on occasions, take the opportunity to close my eyes and relax into a meditative state.

The red-light pod is a full lay-down pod where the entire body is exposed to healing light. Countless studies from universities across the world show everything from fat loss, cellulite improvement, stimulating collagen production, reduction in wrinkles, pain relief, healing skin conditions, improving fibromyalgia and chronic fatigue, brain function, eye and oral health, promotes hair growth, helps reduce inflammation in the body and more. Any wonder many skin clinics and day spas offer different versions and applications of red light therapy on their treatment menus.

Both therapies focus on detoxing and stimulating healing.

FULVIC HUMIC ACID: This is probably one of the most valuable products to have in your at-home pharmacy arsenal due to its powerful cellular healing benefits. I have used it for the entirety of my healing process with zero intention of stopping.

I felt my hair grew back faster than I imagined, my skin regained its glow, and of course, it has helped me with the constant daily detoxing from the medications.

Why did I take it and what are its main health benefits?

- It may reduce inflammation and boost immunity
- May protect brain function, improves brain health, can improve outcomes after traumatic brain injury and reduce swelling and inflammation
- May improve cholesterol levels
- May increase muscle strength
- May help in cellular function and detoxification
- May induce cancer cell death and prevent the spread of certain cancer cells
- May improve gut health by enhancing nutrient absorption and improving certain gut disorders
- May boost testosterone levels – obviously this one is more for the men reading this or partners

Whilst I am an Holistic Health and Wellness Coach, I am not a doctor, so I encourage you to speak with your family GP, a local naturopath, integrative medical practitioner, specialist or pharmacist, especially if you are taking other supplements or medications, as this can cause cellular detoxification, therefore may have side effects. Please do your own research and due diligence for your specific needs.

VITAMINS: Organic high strength Zinc, Liposomal C (after a lengthy initial wait period), magnesium spray/oil applied in the morning usually to the shoulders and at night (before bed) mainly on the stomach, calves and under the feet. The general rule with magnesium oils and sprays is – upper half of the body in the mornings and lower half at night. B-Epics Detox and B-Epics Sleep formula were also incorporated and reintroduced into my routine after approximately 9 months.

WATER: Alka Power – From the time I was discharged from the hospital this is all I drank. Chanel included. I also used Pureau for my kettle water as this was my main water source prior to diagnosis. Why?

Our bodies are predominantly made up of water. We need water to function efficiently daily and of course, to flush out toxins from our cells, organs and lymphatics. There are many other brands on the market depending on where you live, as well as some amazing, fixed water filters and stand-alone filtration systems for homes. Most brands of bottled/packaged water are either neutral or have low pH levels, so I was specifically looking for high alkalinity, zero fluoride and zero heavy metals, and infused with minerals and electrolytes. Ionised water is also an amazing choice.

Now, the final and following two combinations were from my own investigative research into cancer, and specifically metastatic melanoma. Many cancer groups advocate Fenbenzodol (FenBen for short), Ivermectin and others, however I was unable to take these due to contraindications with the chemo tablets. Additionally, I researched several other alternative therapies, however none of them at the time really landed with my intuition and soul guidance.

Around this time, I was beginning to feel anxious, as I had to make a hard decision on the immunotherapy (that I declined) and needed to have a pretty amazing backup plan. So, as I kept the faith that everything would be revealed to me at the perfect time, I continued searching and researching, until one day, I clicked on a link (don't even ask me where it came from, it just divinely appeared on my computer screen), that led me to discover the following two combinations TOGETHER.

Your intuition and higher self are always guiding you. TRUST THEM.

Some of the following information may be rather challenging for you to understand re the terminology, so if you, or a loved one are currently facing a cancer diagnosis, please consult your oncologist and treatment specialists to discuss. These were cleared for me to take in unison with the medication.

INOSITOL +IP6: The following information is extracted from PubMed regarding the studies done on these supplements supporting positive medical results specifically with Stage 4 melanoma:

"Inositol hexaphosphate (IP6) also called phytic acid is a poly phosphorylated carbohydrate naturally found in cereals, nuts, grains, and high-fibre-containing foods. It has been shown **to inhibit the growth of many different tumour cell lines both in vitro and in vivo like colon, pancreas, liver, prostate, and even melanoma.**

Vitamin B inositol is a precursor of IP6 and another naturally occurring compound with anticancer properties. We present a case report of a patient with metastatic melanoma who declined traditional therapy and opted to try over the counter supplement IP6+inositol instead. To our surprise, the patient achieved a complete remission and remains in remission 3 years later.

On the basis of this case and previous preclinical studies, we believe further research is indicated in exploring antiproliferative and potential immune stimulating effects of IP6+inositol in patients with metastatic melanoma.

Inositol hexaphosphate plus inositol induced complete remission in stage IV melanoma: a case report - PubMed (nih.gov)

To explain these findings in simpler terms, IP-6 helps to drain energy from the cancer cells. It seems to do this by preventing crucial cell machinery from being constructed in the first place. Without the right machinery, the cancer cells can't grow or spread as quickly. Next, we'll look at the anti-inflammatory power of IP-6's partner, inositol.

Recent research suggests that inositol influences cell signals involved with inflammation. Inositol may synergize with IP-6's anticancer effects by playing an anti-inflammatory role.

An inflammatory cytokine known as interleukin-6 is over-produced by most cancer cells. The high levels of interleukin-6 seem to have important roles in tumour formation and metabolism, and also function to protect cancer cells from damage.

One of the biggest obstacles with conventional cancer treatments is the risk of harmful side effects. Many chemotherapy drugs can lower the body's production of blood cells. This can lead to major concerns, such as anaemia, excessive bleeding, and/or a weakened immune system. The good news is that some natural substances have shown protective benefits as defence against some cancer treatment side effects.

A small study published in 2010 compared two groups of women with breast cancer who received chemotherapy treatment after surgery. The experimental group received standard chemotherapy in addition to "low-dose" IP-6 + inositol (6 grams, divided into two doses daily). The control group received standard chemotherapy with a placebo [19]. (In this experiment, a vitamin C capsule was used as a placebo. Typically, a placebo contains no active ingredient.)

After 6 months of treatment, this study found that the experimental group (who received IP-6 + inositol) reported having a significantly improved quality of life compared to the control (placebo) group. Comparatively, the women who took IP-6 + inositol with chemotherapy gained the following benefits [20]:

- The group who took IP-6 + inositol had no drop in white blood cells. This shows that their immune system remained stronger.
- The group who took IP-6 + inositol had no reduction in platelets. This shows that they didn't have an increased risk of bleeding.
- The group who took IP-6 + inositol had improved functional status, were better able to perform their daily activities, and enjoyed a better quality of life, based on self-reported surveys.

IP-6 + Inositol May Help You Fight Cancer And Protect Against Chemo Side Effects (anticancer360.com)

The following is also information extracted from a study done in 2021 from the Queen Mary University of London:

> **"IP-6, or inositol hexaphosphate, an antioxidant found in high fibre foods, may slow down the production**

of cancer cells, inhibiting cancers such as prostate cancer, brain cancer and breast cancer by blocking several pathways including mTor and P13K-Akt, and stealing essential iron from cancer cells, starving them of growth; it also may improve chemotherapy effectiveness and reduce side-effects.

How to stop cancer feeding?

In 2021, researchers from Queen Mary University of London 'stopped' a type of **brain cancer,** (Medulloblastoma), common in children, from feeding. How did they do it? They gave the test animals IP-6, found in high fibre foods like bran and whole grain rice, alongside a B vitamin called inositol.

This had two main effects. It chelated to the iron in the cancer cells, (it 'stole' it from the cancer cells), thus stopping them feeding. At the same time, it promoted the *p21* and *p53* genes back towards full power (9).

IP-6 also seems capable of increasing AMPK levels, in turn depressing cancer promoters mTor and Akt."

Is IP-6 a cure for cancer? | CANCERactive

Other evidence-based benefits of taking this supplement may include reducing anxiety, aiding blood sugar control by insulin sensitivity, improving fertility in women with PCOS, reducing symptoms of depression and has a great safety record, with virtually zero side effects.

5 Evidence-Based Health Benefits of Inositol (healthline.com)

There are literally dozens and dozens of articles online that can be accessed if you are guided to research this combination further, for whatever health reason. Please always consult your integrative doctor or specialist, especially if you are already taking supplements or other prescribed medications.

BERBERINE:

> "Berberine (BBR) has been extensively studied in vivo and vitro experiments. BBR inhibits cell proliferation by regulating cell cycle and cell autophagy and promoting cell apoptosis. BBR also inhibits cell invasion and metastasis by suppressing EMT (epithelial-to-mesenchymal transition) and down-regulating the expression of metastasis-related proteins and signalling pathways.

In addition, BBR inhibits cell proliferation by interacting with microRNAs and suppressing telomerase activity. BBR exerts its anti-inflammation and antioxidant properties, and also regulates tumour microenvironment. This review emphasised that BBR as a potential anti-inflammation and antioxidant agent, also as an effective immunomodulator, is expected to be widely used in clinics for cancer therapy.

Cancer is a major cluster of diseases that seriously affects human health. Therefore, development of strategies to prevent and treat cancer is critical.[1] Berberine (BBR), a small molecule isoquinoline alkaloid extracted from the rhizomes of coptis chinensis and hydrastis canadensis, is traditionally used to treat bacterial diarrhea.[2] Recent studies showed that BBR reduced lipid levels and glycemic index, and exerted anti-tumor effects.[3-7] BBR lowered lipid levels via competitive inhibition of HMG-CoA reductase, and by interacting with the 3'-UTR of the LDL receptor (LDLR) to improve the stability of LDLR mRNA.[8]

In vivo experiment showed that BBR alleviated non-alcoholic fatty liver by activating SIRT3.[9] In foam cells, BBR promoted cholesterol efflux by increasing ROS production, and induced autophagy by inhibiting mTOR and Akt phosphorylation.[10] The mechanisms of the hypoglycemic effects of BBR have also been studied extensively.

Studies showed that BBR improved insulin action through inhibition of mitochondrial and activation of AMPK.[11,12] In liver and muscle cells, BBR restored insulin sensitivity by up-regulating InsR expression.[13] In vitro experiments showed that BBR affected glucose uptake by down-regulating miR29-b and increasing Akt expression.[14]

Recent studies have shown that BBR exerted anti-tumor effects against lung cancer, cervical cancer, liver cancer, leukaemia, and other malignancies.[15-18]

BBR inhibits cancer cell proliferation through various mechanisms. Here, in this review, we discussed the effects of BBR on cell cycle, cell apoptosis, cell autophagy, ability of inhibiting cell invasion and proliferation, expression of microRNA, telomerase activity, and tumour microenvironment. Currently, BBR is widely used in basic research and clinical trials. This review clarified the potential of BBR as an anti-cancer drug, which may speed up its clinical application and eventually benefit cancer patients."

In all, BBR inhibits cell invasion and metastasis by affecting the expression of tumour-related signalling pathways and proteins.

The Anti-Cancer Mechanisms of Berberine: A Review (nih.gov)

Outside of an alternative treatment for cancer, Berberine has other health benefits that may include supporting normal blood sugar levels, supporting the immune system, antioxidant and targets inflammation in the body, helps with PCOC's, heart health and cholesterol, provides liver protection and supports gut health, just to name a few.

••

"Think for yourself. Trust your own intuition. Another's mind isn't walking your journey, you are." – Scottie Waves

••

And there you have it. A summary of the therapies and supplements I used. I dedicate another upcoming chapter to my protocol from morning till evening so you can see how I integrated and incorporated these supplements into my day.

I became a master at timing supplements and medications to give my body the ultimate opportunity to heal. Of course, when it comes to detoxing and healing there are many more supplements such as zeolite, colloidal silver, hydrogen peroxide, MSM, black seed oil, essiac tea, mushroom blends, glutathione, liposomal/intravenous C and the list continues but of course, it all depends upon your unique health and healing journey.

Always consult your integrative health practitioner or naturopath before incorporating anything new into your protocol.

MIRACLE INSPIRATION: Your ENTIRE environment CREATES your health.

What you eat, what you drink, what you listen to, what you watch, what you speak, what you think and are surrounded by, on a daily basis.

Trust your intuition.

Energy healing, using specific frequencies, is one of the best ways of releasing the built-up emotional and physical stress, free your body and your mind of the old garbage most likely slowing you down, impacting other areas of your life or literally, as in my case, causing DIS-ease in the body.

All supplements also carry a unique vibration so ensure that whatever you are currently taking is of the highest and purest quality, organic, preferably low to zero fillers and where possible, is either in liquid, powder or dropper form for faster and more effective absorption.

"The treatments themselves do not 'cure' the condition, they simply restore the body's self-healing ability." ~ Leon Chaitow

Chapter 12

HEALING HELP FROM HEAVEN AND EARTH – ANGELS + CRYSTALS AND DIVINE NUMBER SYNCHRONICITIES

••

"You'll meet more angels on a winding path than on a straight one." Terri Guillemets

••

I have mentioned this statement a few times throughout this book, and I will say it again – there is not just one way, and I passionately back this when it comes to health and wellness and healing. Now more than ever, there is a multitude of options, across various alternative modalities that can ASSIST the body to heal or expedite healing, generate higher levels of wellness, aid in boosting the body's ability to remain in a high state of vibration, alongside (and in a lot of cases instead of) general western procedures and medicines.

Tapping into divine source energy and connecting with the angelic realm is one of the most profound ways to feel more at peace when we are anxious, needing more calm when life is chaotic and feeling more balanced when the world around us is in turmoil.

> "Sometimes the most productive thing you
> can do is rest and let your angels wrap you in
> their loving wings. They've got you covered."
> Anna Taylor

My connection to angels began when I was young, however my full awareness of their presence and protective healing power has been highlighted and amplified with age. Following the radiation, my psychic and intuitive senses heightened, which in turn cultivated a closer angelic connection and more tapped in communication with my soul team who watch over me.

Archangel Michael is one of the most prominent Archangels. He can be in multiple places simultaneously and is basically my angelic bodyguard. Apart from God/Spirit, Archangel Michael has protected me, guided me, and helped me through the entirety of this journey.

Throughout my medical appointments I felt his presence through signs, songs and what can only be described as undeniable divine synchronicities. I have NO doubt that there is a Higher Power, higher dimensional heavenly guides and an army of angels watching over each of us. All we must do is ASK for their help.

> "Calling upon the angels when we are in
> need, helps the angels fulfil their heavenly
> mission. We are truly co creators with them."
> Eileen Anglin

They simply cannot help us if we do not ASK.

There are many Archangels, such as Archangel Raphael, who is the angelic physician and healer. Together with Archangel Michael, they regularly accompanied me through all medical appointments, PET and CT scans,

MRI scans and blood tests, and their angelic presence was felt in every consult or treatment room I walked into.

As for intervention and assistance from Heaven, I am simply sharing who is around me or who I call upon specifically, outside of God, the Divine Creator.

Archangel Michael – The Holy Fighter and Warrior – any wonder he is always with me to protect, guide and watch over my family and friends. He can be with countless people all at the same time and is quite literally God's kicker of asses! His energy is that of fiery blue light and is incredibly powerful, cutting through fear, negativity and other dense vibrations such as doubt and distortion.

There is no problem too big or too small for this Archangel and he will always answer your call for help. Anytime you need him, be prepared to feel an energetic shift around you as he shows up for duty or you may feel his strong presence in your immediate surroundings. White feathers and goosebumps when calling his name are personal signifiers of his divine presence around me.

Archangel Raphael - The Divine Physician - Archangel Raphael's name literally means, "He who heals", therefore he is the one to call upon to assist when facing a health crisis or illness, as well as any other spiritual challenges. His famous emerald green healing light will help rejuvenate your physical vitality, break up toxic energy, distortions and blockages to facilitate your body's ability to self heal.

I invoke Archangel Raphael to accompany me to any scans, tests and medical appointments. He is well known as the Archangel who helps and supports those who desire to heal themselves so they can be of a higher service to others and humanity as a whole. He is also known to work closely with those who are called to work and practice in healing modalities, such as energy healers, health coaches, integrative doctors and other wellness practitioners, by sending intuitive guidance and flashes of insight on health issues that patients are struggling with.

Archangel Gabriel – The Messenger Angel – goes without saying that Gabriel often accompanies and assists those in the creative worlds such as writers, teachers, musicians, artists and helping parents in all facets of conceiving to raising children. Archangel Gabriel's messages are a high, divine frequency that speaks directly to the heart. Therefore this beautiful Archangel will assist you in raising your vibration and connecting you to pure Source energy.

Call upon this mighty Angel for all things related to strength, protection and of course, communication. Archangel Gabriel is one of the highest-ranking Archangels. His name literally means God is my strength and is wonderful to call upon in times of stress, sadness and adversity.

Archangel Metatron – The Archangel of Empowerment – one of the most powerful Archangels. His job is to record a tally of all choices, good and bad, and some refer to this book of life as the Akashic Records. All angels are extremely high vibrational and working with Metatron is often linked to energy cleansing on all levels – physically, mentally, emotionally, and energetically.

Metatron is also linked to a contrast in thinking – from negative thoughts to positive ones, therefore if you are stuck and struggling to shift out of the funk, Metatron is the one to help you.

Of course, there are many Archangels.

I have simply given a small snippet of the most important Archangels that I ask for assistance from and invoke for heavenly support. My intuition has strengthened, along with my faith and trust that my angelic team is always watching over me and guiding my path.

Likewise, I am sure at some stage in your own life you have seen or heard about angel numbers? These are number codes specifically linked to the angelic realm and are the most common form of communication. The most significant number code that many begin to see in the initial stages of awakening is 11:11. It is also a perfect time to make a wish and pay attention to your thoughts when you see this sequence.

If you are beginning to see this number code or it is randomly appearing everywhere around you, Metatron and the angelic realm are most likely trying to get your attention. 11:11 is also a powerful DNA activation code and more and more people are noticing this number sequence as the world awakens and shifts into higher consciousness and ways of being. You are most likely ready to shift onto your path of higher purpose. Congratulations!

"Repeated number codes and sequences will have a specific message for you, answer a question, or let you know that you are simply on the right path."

Number sequences appear everywhere throughout my day, signifying and confirming answers or guidance, but mostly as reassurance that I am being looked after and am on the right path.

If this is a new phenomenon and you are questioning the higher meaning behind these sequences, there are multiple trusted websites decoding Angel Numbers on the internet. I personally recommend and refer to Sacred Scribes Angel Numbers. Virtually all number codes can be referenced on this site. It is a reliable and valued source for those searching for the hidden meaning or messages behind any number sequence.
As I wrote this and looked down at my phone, it was 2:22!

This special number, linked significantly to 2022, encompasses balance, peace, harmony, keeping the faith and standing strong in one's personal truths. I love seeing this sequence as it highlights everything working together for the best in the long term, staying positive and knowing that God is working all things out for our highest good. Always.

Throughout this healing journey I specifically requested to see 777 daily as it is very special to me.

God's number is 7 and amplified by 3 means that one is here to spiritually evolve, be of service in both small and big ways and to use one's soul talent to help bring love, light and healing, not only to oneself, but to the world. Effort and hard work will be rewarded, successes will inspire, teach, and help others by example. It is strongly tied to sharing one's higher learning and spiritual perspectives – a profound and timely message as I write this book and send it out to the world.

Have you noticed repeated number patterns around you? Are you asking certain questions or thinking of specific things when you see them?
Pay attention. At the very least open your mind and research what message they may be trying to communicate to you, regardless of whether it is the first time you are reading about this. I guarantee there will be a personal message in there for you somewhere to give you guidance or confirmation.

Naturally scattered throughout this process, there were moments of withdrawal and retreating, questioning and shrinking back into fear-based thoughts, or worrying HOW all of this was going to play out. Therefore, 777 was, and still is, my special sign that I am on the right path, that everything is exactly as it should be, and I am being divinely guided and protected. This number sequence appeared everywhere around me, and continues to show up daily on number plates, shopping dockets, in window displays, phone numbers, emails and other random places, sometimes multiple times a day, and I always say thank you, thank you, thank you each time.

And then there's crystals.

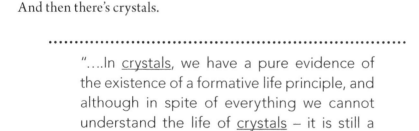

"....In crystals, we have a pure evidence of the existence of a formative life principle, and although in spite of everything we cannot understand the life of crystals – it is still a living being….." – Nikola Tesla

Crystals have been around for thousands of years. And God created all things – including crystals. God never said they were "bad" or "evil". He did say that He must be first place in all things. I feel the confusion and the falsity around these topics comes from those who place them above the Creator in importance and relevance, almost idolising or believing that they in themselves are miracle workers or some holy divinity tool. Crystals are, however, extremely high vibrational, and whilst "science" essentially dismisses their credibility, there are just as many from their own personal experience who say otherwise.

Regardless, Jesus is the Master Healer. Period. There is no other above Him. I do not place greater emphasis on anything else, however crystals carry very high energy and complementary healing abilities that are no longer being dismissed across many different fields.

The beauty industry is also embracing the use of crystals. Everything from facial massage tools to smooth wrinkles on one's face, crushed into face creams and elixirs and used inside the latest water bottles.
There is a definite beauty, a pure vibrational energy, that emanates from these stones that does contribute, compliment and help aid our physical bodies as well as our spiritual bodies. Crystals are also wonderful to work with for chakra balancing, realigning and clearing.

And if you still can't quite wrap your head around any of that, then the bottom line is, they are beautiful to have as decorative pieces around your home or worn as a statement piece in rings, bracelets, earrings, necklaces or body jewellery.

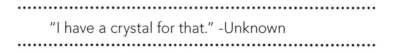

"I have a crystal for that." -Unknown

Throughout my personal healing journey, there are probably 5 crystals that I would virtually never be without to assist in keeping my body protected and shielded, at peace, continue healing and able to tap into my higher self/intuition. Nevertheless, I have listed below the top 10 that I would recommend to those first starting out or those who are looking for a particular crystal or crystals that are multifunctional or just beautiful to wear or have in your home.

1. CLEAR QUARTZ –THE MASTER HEALING CRYSTAL

···

"Quartz is the most powerful healing and energy amplifier on the planet." -Judy Hall

···

I personally prefer larger chunky pieces placed around the home, wearable points, or pendants. Clear quartz is THE most powerful healing and energy amplifying stone amongst all crystals. It is said that this amazing crystal can absorb, amplify and transmute negative energy. As far as health and healing goes, it may also boost the body's immune system and clear and balance out your auric field.

This gorgeous, pure, divine stone cleanses and enhances one's organs and acts as a deep soul cleanser. It will aid concentration and memory and help integrate the mind, body connection. It can amplify the energy of other crystals placed alongside it so you will find it paired in my home with many others mentioned in this list, and as such, is my favourite.

2. SELENITE – THE PEACEMAKER – or as I like to call it "the calming crystal".

My second choice, and another you simply should consider adding to your home environment or wearing on a daily basis. I have gorgeous selenite wands and towers in my bedroom, in the lounge room and Chanel's bedroom. I remember one of my trusted healers visiting my home in the middle of my journey.

She placed her hands on my head and after about 20 seconds said, *"Wow. Your inner body is just so calm. I mean it's totally calm. It's ridiculous. I have never felt this before."*

And I did feel calm.

I knew this was predominantly due to my unwavering faith that God was in control. However I observed noticeable differences in the energy of my home, an elevated sense of calm within myself as well as Chanel by placing strategic pieces in the bedrooms and living areas. On occasions where pressure would build inside my head, I would (and still do), place a selenite wand on my temples or forehead (third eye) and it would often disappear within 10-15 minutes, sometimes sooner.

3. ROSE QUARTZ – THE LOVE CRYSTAL OR HEART HEALER

••

"Rose quartz is said to be the stone of unconditional love. This crystal opens the heart chakra and is believed to encourage self-love and forgiveness, and to help you let go of anger, resentment, and jealousy." - Miranda Kerr

••

It is a gorgeous (and very feminine) companion to clear quartz and when placed together is said to amplify the frequencies and abilities of both. Rose quartz, whilst not only beautiful in colour, is the stone said to aid deepening connections for lovers, partnerships in general, friendships and even our own relationship with ourselves.

And let's face it, it doesn't matter what you are up against right now, there is always more room for more self-love, especially if you are healing - emotionally or physically.

4. CITRINE – THE ABUNDANCE STONE

Said to be the stone for enhancing all things prosperity, money, abundance, health and wealth. This gorgeous golden crystal supposedly sparks your joy, amps up your optimism, motivates you and generally releases negative traits whilst boosting your clarity and motivation levels. It is amazing for releasing deep-seated fears, anger and negative feelings due to its bright yellow gold hues and can awaken your solar plexus to help cultivate more confidence and personal power, and as such, is very popular with men. According to Feng Shui experts, to magnify its effects, it is best placed in the wealth area which is usually in the south-east corner of your home.

5. AMETHYST – THE INTUITIVE STONE

Definitely in the top five of pretty much every crystal lover's kit and probably one of THE most well-known and well recognised crystals, even if you have never entertained a second thought about them in your life! Why is this one extremely popular? It is made from quartz so immediately has strong amplification qualities. Because of this, amethyst can also be programmed. It may assist in opening your third eye and crown chakras to clear your auric field of energetic debris that stands between you and a closer and more accurate level of intuition.

In fact, I would say it is THE stone for increasing intuition, and assisting in connecting to our own higher self. It is incredibly protective and one of the best healing stones. And usually with stressful situations comes sleep deprivation or broken sleep, therefore, unless you are a light sleeper, amethyst is revered as a crystal to improve sleep quality and calm the nervous system. Great for children too. I have pieces near my bed and under my daughter's pillow.

6 TIGERS EYE – THE POWER STONE

Another favourite in my crystal collection and is frequently worn in some form daily.
Tigers Eye may help in increasing confidence and power, and due to the crystal's deep honey brown colour, is also a very popular choice for men. As a compliment to those star qualities, it also boosts creativity, assists with making clear, concise decisions, rids the body and mind of overwhelm, fear, stress and anxiety.

7. BLACK OBSIDIAN – THE DETOXIFICATION STONE

I will be completely honest here. I am rather drawn to most black crystals! Black obsidian has a major affinity with protection, repelling negativity and creating almost like a force field of protection around the wearer's body. Also classed as the crystal of detoxification, it will help the physical body expel toxins of all kinds and help the mental and spiritual body get rid of emotional blockages.

8. BLACK TOURMALINE – THE PROTECTIVE STONE

Well known as a powerful healing and protecting stone, this crystal is used widely by most healers and crystal lovers. It is said to block spiritual attacks and ground a person's energy. I wear it daily.

In recent times with the introduction of WIFI and our obsession with gadgets, it has also become a major player in protecting us from harmful EMF radiation emitting from mobile phones, computers, and our society of tech overload.

9. SHUNGITE – THE SHIELDING STONE

Mainly found and sourced from Russia, this mysterious stone is made up of 99% carbon and is also a popular choice by many in shielding us from harmful electromagnetic waves.

Shungite also consists of nearly all the minerals on the periodic table and is thought to be at least 2 billion years old. Its main benefits include helping kill BACTERIA and VIRUSES, purifying water, reducing oxidative stress in the body, reducing inflammation, and easing physical ailments such as liver and kidney problems, asthma, allergies and more. It is also said that it may improve sleep quality if placed next to your bed.

10. JASPER – THE SUPREME NURTURER

This is like the mother and the BFF of crystals both rolled into one. Jasper also comes in various colours but the most common and popular is red. It is said to empower your spirit, give you the encouragement, confidence, and courage to help tackle the big issues and support you through major times of stress.

So, if you are a crystal lover or have often wondered what the fascination was with them, you can begin to see why I have chosen these as my personal Top 10. They all complement each other, and all have their special place when it comes to elevating your vibration, overcoming adversity and assisting with health and healing on all levels. I have numerous crystals in my home, either in wearable jewellery, small clusters in various bowls around the house, larger chunks or towers beside my bed, in my bathroom and even in my car.

All my crystal lovers out there will agree – you can never have enough crystals!

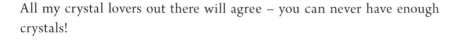

"The thing about my crystal obsession is that it doubles as high-vibe home decor." -Unknown

There are literally dozens of books on crystals outlining their individual and positive healing benefits if this has stirred you on some level to know more.

When friends and strangers ask me what ones to purchase, I simply respond by saying it is the ones that YOU are drawn to. Your eyes will automatically be drawn to the perfect one or one's for you. There are no mistakes. Your soul knows what it needs to assist you along your own journey and especially in times of adversity and challenges. This is also a great way for children to choose and connect with these gorgeous stones and begin to open their own intuitive gifts.

Try it. The next time you walk into a crystal store, just go with the crystals you gravitate towards or the ones you repeatedly feel pulled back to. Most crystal stores (and even online) will supply you with the crystal meanings of each. Whilst I haven't added to my collection recently, I never chose incorrectly in the past and consistently ended up with the perfect crystal for my needs or wishes at the time.

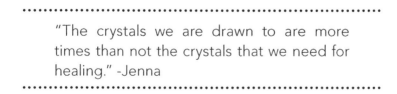

"The crystals we are drawn to are more times than not the crystals that we need for healing." -Jenna

MIRACLE INSPIRATION: Begin to tap into the higher Angelic dimensions. Angels are everywhere. Their ability to communicate to you, whether it's through signs, symbols or sequences is readily available. All you need to do is ASK.

All crystals carry a high vibrational energy and are especially helpful when used in meditations or by placing them strategically in your home or on your body via wearable jewellery. It is also said that you can infuse your crystals with your own mantras or affirmations.

Are you struggling with specific emotions or limitations in your life right now? Write down your own affirmation that best serves what you need at this time. The most important thing to do is clearly ask for what you NEED.

For example – an affirmation to infuse into black tourmaline might be – "I am always protected, and I know I am safe." Or "I let go of all stress and worry in my life because I know everything will be ok."

Regardless of how you choose to use them, always ensure your crystals are regularly cleansed, charged and cleared of old energies or affirmations as needed.

Essentially, if you feel crystals will help support you on an energetic level then go with your intuition. On the other hand, if you believe the opposite and base your views and opinion on science, then that's fine too. You do you.

What is true, is that quartz has the ability to amplify and magnify your thoughts on what you truly want and desire.

Chapter 13

THE MIDDLE CAN BE MESSY - Shit hitting the fan is part of the Plan.

....

"The place of true healing is a fierce place. It's a giant place. It's a place of monstrous beauty and endless dark and glimmering light. And you have to work really, really, really hard to get there, but you can do it." ~ Cheryl Strayed

....

Four days before my 48th birthday I met with another private oncologist. A female. A welcome change from a very male dominated field. She was to be my third opinion on the proposed immunotherapy I had previously rejected and was a referral and recommendation from my private oncologist, Jim. From the first moment she walked out of her office to greet Jay and I, I just knew I was meant to see her.

Over the next one and half hours, we would go through everything from my initial diagnosis, family history, the childhood farm/fertilisers and pesticides connection, the previous surgery to remove a freckle from my back, to the previous and current medications, the radiation, and now, the reason I was there, to discuss the recommended immunotherapy and whether there were ANY other options.

She was compassionate, understanding and delivered her messages and seasoned opinion with clarity, professionalism, and the blunt bottom line.

I respected her unequivocally for that. She talked how I talked. Not always giving me what I wanted to hear but it was direct, backed up with knowledge and frontline personal experience from numerous past and present patients.

Up until that point, I had held my hopes high that she would provide me with the long anticipated "other options", another way, a miracle suggestion that would keep me out of the hospital and protect my body from the harsh synthetic drugs that came with a high chance of severe side effects. Yet as she sat there poker faced, yet still exuding a warmth, she instead read me her cold, blunt bottom line. My face changed from hopeful to having the wind completely knocked out of me – all within the space of minutes.

Her voice echoed with words along the lines of, either do this treatment with a 50% or higher chance of serious side effects, most likely requiring hospitalisation, to possibly long-term permanent damage to the thyroid, organs, most likely the liver, and the body's own immune system, OR face the very in-your-face reality that I may only have between a few months to possibly a year to live if the cells recalibrated and strengthened their resistance. I couldn't look at Jay. Tears were already filling my eyes as she spoke. I sat there numb, frozen and shell-shocked. My positive frame of mind was shattered in a thousand pieces as I grappled with the same dark feelings from only five months earlier at the very beginning of the diagnosis.

How could I be feeling so good? How could the scans and MRI be showing everything was going in the right direction? Heck, some of the clusters had even disappeared completely. How could it be possible for these cells to potentially become resistant, multiply and return even more aggressively? What about Chanel? My parents? They can't bury a third child. At 94 and 89 it would destroy them.

And the big one for me, how could God allow this NOW?

It was like time stood still all over again. A kill shot to my heart. And a kill shot to my mindset. I felt ripped off. I felt as though I had been given false positives and it was all just an illusion. I felt as though

the substantial progress I had achieved and the effort I had put into moving things in the right direction, was instead rapidly propelled backwards, almost free-falling once again without a parachute.

I walked out of her office feeling defeated, as though I had lost my battle before it had even begun. Potentially I was standing on a very real and very dark precipice, as to whether I jumped or not.

It was a cold but sunny winter day outside. I remember feeling the bite in the air, cutting through my jumper like a knife. I felt cold. Not only physically but cold on the inside. Like my heart had been frozen.

In true Jay style, as we walked towards his car, we talked openly and honestly about each scenario. I loved that about him. He got my way of thinking, and I got his. We did not always agree, and neither of us liked hearing the word "no" or "it can't be done", but after 16 years of working together, along with Bee, we had all developed strong, unbreakable, yet brutally honest soul connections. It was black or white. To hell with grey.

The chat helped extract and diffuse the immediate emotional charge and placed me back in my mental mindset. As ironic as it sounds, that was my preferred domain. The source of my pain was also the source of my comfort. Air signs usually find solutions, not emotions. I did not "do" emotions well.

As I drove home, analysing and processing her entire conversation, I was a mixture of tears welling in my eyes at each set of lights, to the usual *"pull yourself together Kath. Stop it. You've got this. It's shit now but you will get through it."*

As I walked through my front door there was a surge of emotional relief. The safety net of home. That solace where I could just be myself, take the hard hat off and just let it all out. I burst into a flood of tears, and they just kept flowing for a good couple of minutes. Then the internal switch flicked, and that inner warrior grit came to the forefront and rationally said *"ok, so you've cried and let it all out. Now what? What else is this really going to achieve right now? Nothing. So, let's get on with it."*

I cannot tell you how many times over the coming hours I fluctuated between tears, total mess and mindset. I listened to Joel Osteen, Tony Robbins, Steve Harvey, music videos, played frequency music through my unit, anything that helped pull me up and out of that negative space. I talked out loud to my guides and angels and I sent a boatload of prayer requests skyward.

I can tell you though, that this ONE pivotal day was the catalyst for this entire chapter of the book. It threw me into the ocean that said sink or swim sweetheart. There ain't no life jackets or lifeguards coming to save you. You have to save yourself. You have to think strategically about how to swim and stay afloat right now to get you to safer ground.

That day was my breaking point.
It was like a cold hard slap to the face where my little bubble of positivity burst, and I was left soaked in reality.
I was basically damned if I did and damned if I didn't.

How you handle the breaking point is what will determine your outcome.
The breaking point is the turning point.
When faced with an adversity, an emotional crisis, a terminal diagnosis, most people will run away, isolate themselves, be filled with fear, accept what is, get too emotional and give up.
So how do you know how the story ends, or how to be a champion, if you have never survived and pushed THROUGH a breaking point?

The difference with a warrior fueled by a winning spirit is not how you handle the start or the finish, but how you handle the MIDDLE.
The mess.
The confusion and the destruction.
The long haul.
When it feels like insurmountable pressure is pushing down HARD on you and it doesn't get easier.
Instead, it's as though the intensity is dialled UP.

How you manage the critical mass in these life-changing and often life-defining moments, will ultimately affect how you come out on the other side. It is in these crucial and pivotal moments of sheer exhaustion, grief, despair and desperation that you must INCREASE your faith, mindset, and discipline within yourself, and trust the process.

Even when no one else can see it.

Perhaps not even you.

The middle is the middle. It is not the end. And if that's all you can extract in your own situation right now, then that's ok. Just know it's the middle and you can survive the middle. You have come this far. Do not give up or give in now.

Perhaps change perspective and ask yourself, is God, Source, Spirit simply processing me?

One of the most profound statements that has anchored in my mind since day one is:

God never uses anyone greatly until He tests them deeply.

When you walk into the storm, you don't know WHEN that storm will end. It can be a few hours, a couple of days, maybe weeks, months or even years.

Not what you want to hear. Not what I wanted to hear.

Whatever is required for your BEST SELF future, God will test you NOW.

Maybe it will be to build more resilience, increase your inner strength, refine your character, build patience. Maybe it is to go through the storm so you can lead others through too, be the example, shed the light, be the way-maker, whatever is needed to bring you into full alignment with your Divine Soul Purpose.

The middle can be messy. It may look like there is no hope, no way out, the relationship is dead in the water, you are going backwards not forwards, the grief is too much to bear, money is tight or non-existent, the medical report says there is no way.

All of us have the stamina and willpower when we first encounter a challenge - and usually at the end - when we see the finish line in front of us. But not too many people talk about HOW to stay consistent, inspired, strong and determined in the middle. Because none of us know exactly how long we are going to spend there in that uncomfortable, uncertain, shaky, sometimes heartbreaking, and soul-destroying place.

Whatever you are facing though, know this, there is an END.
Nothing stays the same.
Everything is always in a state of change.
EVERYTHING.

Sometimes that change can arrive quickly. Other times it can feel as though you are climbing mountain after mountain after mountain with no peak in sight. Your body is tired. Your soul is tired. The weight is too much to bear. It feels like there is absolutely nothing happening with no glimmer of hope or positivity anywhere around you. The grinding and pushing is RELENTLESS. The motivation has left the building. The disinterest has set in. The dream, the goal, the vision seems to be further away than ever before. The monkey mind begins to whisper, "What's the point? It's never going to happen."

Don't make the setbacks be the excuse to throw in the towel.
ACTION conquers FEAR every time.
Make adjustments if you have to, but just keep going.
Keep moving forward.
One foot in front of the other.
One minute at a time.
One hour at a time.
One day at a time.

Whatever it takes to move you THROUGH the present messy moment and not look or falter backwards.
If you are facing something big right now, or have just come through something life-changing, you've probably had enough, said enough, done enough and you are most likely tired.

I hear you.

And I surely feel you.

But please – DO NOT STOP.

AND DO NOT GIVE UP.

"You didn't come this far, to just come this far."

MIRACLE INSPIRATION: Stay focused on the FINISH line, not the middle of the race.

You must MASTER your breaking point.

Because this is where you either give up or push through to the other side!

Lift yourself.

Be there for yourself.

However that looks for you.

Speak kind words.

Be gentle.

Be patient.

Love yourself harder.

Praise yourself for all your effort and energy in getting here, to this very point.

Be understanding. Be all of these things to yourself.

Be your own best friend.

You will have good days but allow yourself to have less than good days.

Everybody does.

I definitely did. And I most definitely still do.

Just find whatever it is you need to pull yourself UP and OUT of the shadow energy because brighter days are ahead of you.

Setbacks, spinning the wheels and failures will have most people convince themselves to give up.

You are meant to lead a loving, meaningful and purposeful life.

None of us are getting out of here alive so conduct your life like you would your job or business.

With grit, goals, and determination to see it through.

I can't do this work for you. No one can. Only YOU can change your thoughts, your perspective, your mindset, your approach and ultimately your decision to APPLY and consistently DO what I have passionately written in this book. And most importantly – following what is in your HEART and SOUL.

What would your future self say to you right now?

"Tough times don't last, but tough people do.

Chapter 14

EVERYDAY GRATITUDE -
the simple things are usually
the most beautiful things

"If the only prayer you said was thank you, that would be enough."— Meister Eckhart

Every morning when I wake up the first words out of my mouth, before my feet even hit the floor, is THANK YOU, THANK YOU, THANK YOU. Thank you God for blessing me with another day, thank you for my healing, thank you for everything I have, everyone I love and thank you for all the blessings still to come.

I am affirming and declaring and speaking gratitude each day for simply being alive! For my breath. For another day on this earth. Another day that I have with my beautiful daughter, another day with my friends, another day helping people through my work, another day meeting people from all walks of life, another day for our protection and guidance and another day for the opportunity to be of service to those I meet, interact with, and speak with.

I have always been grateful for the little things, but this journey took it to the next level. Deep, meaningful gratitude, and I mean the gratitude that stirs your soul, or maybe even brings a tear to your eyes, when you are truly humbled by even the simplest things. THAT is the essence and true power of gratitude.

It is one thing to SAY you are grateful, but it is another to actually FEEL it, and honestly thank God, the Universe, Source, Angels, Spirit and MEAN it. And I honestly feel that most of us don't truly understand this until we personally experience a life-defining moment, an unexpected challenge or shocking adversity that redefines how we truly look at our lives, what we have - and WHO we have.

When was the last time you woke up in the morning and said, *"Thank you for waking me up today, thank you for my sight, thank you for my hearing, thank you for my touch, my taste, my arms, my legs, thank you that I can walk and talk? Thank you for the roof over my head, thank you for my clothes, thank you for hot water, running water, any water, thank you that my family and friends are safe, thank you for food in my fridge, thank you for electricity, thank you for my car, thank you that all my bills are paid and all my needs are met?"*

This is such a simple list but also possibly the most humble and sincere. Of course, you can say thank you for ANY thing in ANY way that resonates with you. For most of us however, the simple things are not even thought about in our busy, distracted daily routines because most are waiting to be grateful for the big stuff - the bigger house, the new car, the amazing career, the holiday, the cash in the bank, the business success, the perfect person. We almost take these unimaginably important things for granted, or they are readily dismissed as insignificant. Yet take any of these vitally important and fundamental basics away and our lives would be radically different.

In adversity, it is so easy to draw ourselves to the negative, the situation at hand, the problem, the turmoil, shock, sadness, grief, anger, frustration that we forget about all the things that are still going RIGHT, that are still ok, that are still working and functioning and solid in our lives. If you struggle to find things to be grateful for, perhaps begin by expressing gratitude right now for the fact that you are still BREATHING.

Yes, of course we are all humans, feeling all the emotional feels, and that is ok, that is healthy when expressed, however I would often pull myself up in moments of good old self-pity or exhaustion and remind myself that I have so much to be grateful for at any given moment and that this too shall pass.

About 6 months into my journey, I reconnected with an amazingly gifted woman who was a trusted source for kinesiology sessions. I had known her for many years both personally and through a private group for those choosing to live a more holistic lifestyle. I recall being drawn this particular day to one of the group posts. Something triggered intuitively inside of me to reach out and touch base. Initially, I treaded softly, outlining my situation very simply and continued to update her of my progress over the course of about a month. Her compassion and kindness and offers of support truly touched me. I felt drawn to visit her for another kinesiology session and allow her to "do her thing".

Now her healing techniques at the time were quite expansive and impressive, and my internal voice kept repeating *"just go see her"*. The moment we finally caught up it was a delayed emotional trigger, having to reaffirm the diagnosis, pull up scans, my treatments, and for the very first time, talk about how I was FEELING – not just FUNCTIONING. Essentially everything. Because that's what I had been doing – simply functioning on adrenaline. There was an immediate flood of uncontrollable tears out of nowhere as I began speaking about the initial shock, Chanel, the story thus far, yet simultaneously feeling as though I was detached and talking about a third party.

It was a trauma response I had unconsciously encompassed to get me through, keep me focused and moving forward, and so, the cathartic tears were a welcome relief to my exhausted soul. Her session was a combination of kinesiology and body communication, leaving me rather tired afterwards as it released stuck energy in muscles and different parts of my body, however I slept well and felt amazing the next day!

Whilst in her company, she offered, (actually more like insisted), that she write a post anonymously to the private group for support, offers of service and anything else the members felt led to give. I didn't know what to say except THANK YOU. I wasn't expecting it. I felt I didn't "need" it but as I read her post days later, I teared up again. How WE interpret our challenges is often not how OTHERS perceive it. Again, I felt like I was reading someone else's story, so surreal, yet beautifully compassionate and empathetic.

The response was overwhelming. Tears fell reading the genuinely beautiful and thoughtful comments from virtual strangers, as well as familiar group members I had interacted with here and there, occasionally commenting on posts to give words of wisdom, advice and support. Yet here these kind and generous souls were, out of the warmth of their own hearts, offering services, groceries, holiday getaways, treatments and of course, words of encouragement, strength and divine healing. I was overcome and shocked by the touching response, and whilst I was beyond appreciative, I graciously and humbly declined most of their offers as there were others far more in need than me.

Within a few days however, I received yet another beautiful surprise. As Chanel and I stepped out of the lift and walked to our front door, there on the floor were two large boxes of organic fruits, vegetables, nuts, seeds and pantry items from one of the very generous businesses associated with the group. For me, it was like Christmas! Forget perfumes and all the usual girly things. The biggest smile along with feelings of complete overwhelm and surprise spread across my face at these boxes overflowing with everything my body needed. Feelings of *"how can I accept all of this? I don't need this? This should be going to others who are truly in need."*
Yet this beautiful gesture, not only made an enormous impact on me, but also an enormous impact on my level of appreciation and gratitude.
God, Source, Universe, whoever and whatever you label that higher force, was simply showing me what I DESERVED.

Yes, I was "totally fine", but God was bringing these people to me at this particular time to show me more love, more support and more kindness and a beautiful reminder that there are in fact, still so many generous people with kind hearts in the world and I wasn't alone.

These complete strangers wanted to see me WIN by supporting me in whatever way they could. And again, my level of gratitude INCREASED.
I remember going to bed that night rather awe-struck and shocked that so many people felt so strongly about helping ME. It was a huge check-in emotionally on where my mindset was at. I had been so self-sufficient, so "fine", so capable, so fiercely independent for such a long time and so used to giving back in various ways to others, that I had forgotten the fine art of RECEIVING.

> "A grateful heart is a magnet for miracles."
> Sarah Prout

These kind and generous offers were simply ADDING to the outpouring of support from Jay and Bianca, my work colleagues, family and close friends.

You can protect yourself, but most importantly, you can protect your mind from negativity, the more you layer it in gratitude. Just imagine for a moment that your mind is coated in Teflon and the Teflon is gratitude. Nothing negative can stick. Every day we want to ensure that the Teflon coating on our mind is layered with gratitude and THANK-FUL-NESS. Even for the little things. Remember, there is someone, somewhere, who WISHES they had your life. There is always someone doing it tougher than you. NO matter what you are going through, there is always something to be grateful for.

You will be far better equipped at handling the bad days, the shitty job, the relationship turmoil, the sudden change in events, if your mind is coated in GRATEFULNESS.

The more grateful and thankful you are, for anything and ALL things, the more life will begin to FLOW. Yes there may be turbulence, however if you are predominantly displaying and cultivating gratitude, then vibrationally, you will begin to ATTRACT more ease, joy and happiness into your life. In those times of turmoil or chaos, you will be far better equipped at staying calm and flowing with life, rather than pushing against it.
I for one want more of all of that, and I am certain that you do too.

Everyday I am grateful for the little things. This journey has opened my eyes to what truly matters in life and what I truly have – and that is LIFE, vibrant health, beautiful friendships, a peaceful and protected home environment, laughter, joy, love, and Divine favour, blessings, protection and guidance over myself and Chanel.

Every day in every way, all of my needs are met. How blessed and grateful am I!

MIRACLE INSPIRATION: Right now, in this very moment, no matter what your story or purpose for being here, what are 3 people, places or things that you are TRULY grateful for in your life? In other words, if these people or these things weren't in your life tomorrow how would that make you feel and how would that IMPACT your life?

What level of GRATITUDE do you openly have for them?
Is this gratitude authentically expressed regularly?

The old saying, *"you don't know what you've got until it's gone"* typically rings true when we lose people we love, things that we took for granted and time that we can never recapture.

When we begin to develop a DEEP appreciation and gratitude for the little things in life, including the people who are a part of it, not only does this create a substantial lift in your own mood, as well as make others feel good, it also AMPLIFIES and E-X-P-A-N-D-S the energy behind it.

Appreciate life and it will begin to appreciate you.

•••

"Everyone enjoys being acknowledged and appreciated. Sometimes even the simplest act of gratitude can change someone's entire day. Take the time to recognize and value the people around you and appreciate those who make a difference in your lives."— Roy T. Bennett

•••

Chapter 15

FOOD IS FUEL AND FREQUENCY
– YOU ARE WHAT YOU EAT

And what you consume in all forms

••

"Tell me what you eat, and I will tell you what
you are." Anthelme Brillat-Savarin

••

This is probably my domain. I have lived and breathed this for over 25
years. Did I always get it right? No. Do I always get it right now? Heck no!
I definitely know better NOW, but if I do slip up, or have a "cheat" day, (or
days), it is coming from complete conscious awareness.
It is my CHOICE.

Michael Pollan said it best, "You are what you eat." And if asked about food,
you would probably answer there are three main food groups – protein, fats
and carbohydrates. And you would be correct. However, this elevates to a
whole new level when you begin to break down the energetic VIBRATION
and FREQUENCY of the food you are ingesting – and the vibration and
frequency with which it is grown, made, manufactured and CONSUMED.

Remember – over and over again - everything is energy. The lower the frequency, the less LIFE FORCE energy and the less nutritional and health benefit it is to your body.

ZERO exceptions.

A healthy body will usually vibrate at a frequency between 62-68Hz.

Illness and dis-ease begins to manifest in the body when the body's frequency drops below 58Hz.

Colds and flus usually manifest when the body's frequency drops to 57-60Hz.

The body becomes susceptible to cancer at around 42Hz.

Death is around 28Hz.

Therefore, if the human body is vibrating CONSISTENTLY lower than 58Hz this is where most health issues MANIFEST into serious or long-term issues.

When it comes to healing – on any level – but especially healing from sickness or disease - the QUALITY of the food you are consuming is a very important part of the puzzle. As with words, thoughts and your immediate environment, everything you are eating (and drinking) is either taking you towards perfect divine health or further away from it.

This is why those who advocate a healthy lifestyle and are all about clean food, exercise and quality sleep, are predominantly positive in mindset and disposition. Whether they understand the concept or not, it is essentially a form of high vibrational living!

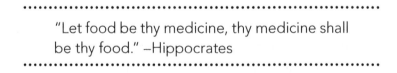

> "Let food be thy medicine, thy medicine shall
> be thy food." –Hippocrates

My biggest awakening around food, frequency and lifestyle came whilst studying holistic health and nutrition in 2011. After learning the truth about my then favourite brand name protein powders, skincare, makeup, household products and no sugar/low sugar treats, I essentially binned them all. Once you learn something, you can ignore it, however you can't unlearn it. I realised my environment, whilst on the surface level appeared healthy, was in actual fact, a chemical shitstorm in disguise. This was a major life defining moment.

As I began to coach, educate and inspire clients, colleagues and friends and other people around me, I would often begin by having them choose any food product in their home. If you did the same thing right now, any packaged food product at all, and turned it over to the ingredients label, would you recognise every single ingredient on the list? More importantly, would your BODY recognise every single ingredient? What about the food items in your pantry, fridge or freezer?

In addition to that, are the equally important household and personal care products. Are you applying, or using, or consuming products that are essentially a science lab filled with synthetically engineered ingredients? I know I was!

I believed my lifestyle was a billboard for health, yet under the microscope, most of what I was eating at the time, as well as using on my body and around the home, was a chemical wasteland.

I vividly recall in my early days of studying, the amazing opportunity of speaking with Miranda Kerr's mother - Theresa Kerr - founder of The Divine Company. Her backstory was also rather incredible.

In 2001 Theresa discovered tumours growing in her spleen. One of her integrative specialists at the time requested she write down every product that was used on a daily basis, along with the list of ingredients in each one. She explained to me this was the catalyst. It blew her mind. In a nutshell, her body was swimming in chemicals that it simply couldn't process quickly or eliminate effectively and efficiently. This was her life-defining moment to begin researching her own answers, encompassing a more holistic lifestyle, and ultimately was the backstory behind the creation of her gorgeous DIVINE organic products, walking in the footsteps of her famous daughter, Miranda and her own KORA range.

Remember – if your body cannot filter out the daily load of toxins, these chemicals will continue to circulate around the body and eventually end up in the ORGANS.

One of the most profound statistics in our conversation that day was - the average FEMALE applies approximately 70 chemicals to her FACE (not including the body) every single day before she even walks out the door, with a combined mix of cleansers, toners, serums, moisturisers and make-up, and uses approximately 12 products every day on her face and body, with an average of 515 chemicals combined. Seriously.

This isn't including the food she is consuming at all - simply applying to her face and her body! Now multiply that by however many days a week, every month, 12 months a year and then by the number of years using these, or other products. Think that is scary? What about our children and newborn babies?

*"Of the more than 400 chemicals tested for, **287** were detected in umbilical cord blood. Of these, 180 cause cancer in humans or animals, 217 are toxic to the brain or nervous system, and 208 cause birth defects or abnormal development in animals. Scientists refer to the presence of such toxins in the newborn as "body burden."*

Study finds hundreds of toxic chemicals in umbilical cords of newborns - World Socialist Web Site (wsws.org)

But that is a book for another day!

Let's refocus on food. If I asked you to write down everything you ate in one day, along with the ingredients for each, would it be healthy, simple and recognisable, or would it be a shopping list of numbers, additives, fast foods, packet foods, tinned foods, preservatives, flavour enhancers, hydrogenated fats, sugar and more?

What a lot of us PERCEIVE as healthy, thanks to words, pretty packaging and rather deceptive marketing, is anything but healthy. Even the "health foods"! Most packaged foods are a chart of numbers or filled with artificial ingredients that our bodies simply DO NOT recognise. If a food label has more than 5 ingredients (unless made from whole food products) then seriously question its health rating or whether it truly deserves a place in your trolley - and most importantly, in your BODY!

Remember, the vast majority of our food items did not exist 50 years ago. And neither did the high rates of cancers, behavioural issues in our children, inflammatory diseases, poor gut health, and a host of other health issues. Yes, there are many other contributing factors, however our increasing appetite for processed, packaged and fast foods is unequivocally a major contributing factor.

For those of you who have never thought about this before and feel confused or unsure, the easiest and simplest way to initially read a food label is - the first ingredient is the MAIN ingredient – and then in descending order from there.

And every ingredient has its own VIBRATION and FREQUENCY.

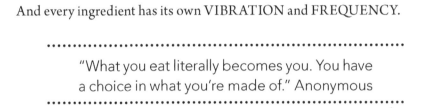

"What you eat literally becomes you. You have
a choice in what you're made of." Anonymous

I would regularly remind clients that as children we are not born wanting junk foods. They are often GIVEN to us by parents or caregivers, usually when we are young as a REWARD or a treat. We then develop cravings because these "treats" have been designed to hook us via chemical reactions in the brain, yet our physical bodies don't need them to LIVE.

We wonder as a society why we now have this endless selection of products on our supermarket shelves, yet our true health collectively, is at serious levels of disease, illnesses, obesity and is essentially anything but vibrant.

For the most part, packaged foods are literally designed in laboratories to ensure the consumer becomes addicted to certain ingredients (or combinations of ingredients), to ensure they return for more.

FACT.

Repeat customers = repeat revenue.

These are basic business principles.

••

> "Any food that requires enhancing by the use
> of chemical substances should in no way be
> considered a food." – John H. Tobe

••

I would often spend time conducting private supermarket tours with working women, busy mothers and professionals, educating them on how to navigate the grocery aisles, what to buy, what to leave and what to substitute, or swap out, for their old family favourites. It was an eye-opener, yet set them up for better CHOICES, as they became educated and empowered to read any label quickly and then DECIDE whether the product was a good choice for themselves and/or their families.

Once you possess the ability to decipher and read a label, ANY label, related to food, household products and personal care items it is an absolute game changer! I would observe their reactions as I dissected their popular product labels into tangible, understandable and relatable health facts.

Instead of standing in the grocery aisle with a confused or blank expression, wondering if the product in their hands was or wasn't "ok", wasting valuable time and energy mulling over the labels because of deceptive wording or a string of numbers instead of names, they now had the tools and the KNOWLEDGE to quickly make that decision, or search for healthier options themselves. For these busy and health conscious individuals, it was extremely empowering to realise this could be done pretty much anytime, anywhere, and with any product.

It is no coincidence that many brand name products are less expensive than the eco, natural, healthier options, as they are predominantly filled with cheap and nasty ingredients, that essentially means cheap and nasty for you!

Of course, the next layer or level to this is the FREQUENCY or vibration of the products placed in the trolley or basket. Imagine you drive your dream car, whatever that is – would you fill it with the cheapest fuel, or would you fill it with premium? Most sensible people would, of course, fill it with the best possible fuel. Premium car = premium fuel.

Now imagine that your dream car is your BODY, and the "fuel" is the FOOD you are filling it with.
Every single thing you are consuming is either slowly destroying the body's engine, or it is maintaining its optimal condition.
Everything you put in your mouth, you (predominently) get to CHOOSE. Just like the fuel in your dream car.

> "When the diet is wrong, medicine is of no use. When diet is correct, medicine is of no need". – Ayurvedic Proverb

Of course, the goal is perfect vibrant health. Therefore, you may understand why when the diagnosis came back, I was in complete disbelief. Leading up to that defining moment, I felt I was the human billboard for health! I had predominently lived and breathed a consistently healthy lifestyle.

However, my INTERNAL VIBRATION for years and years prior, was anything but healthy. It was vibrating constantly in the danger zone as I navigated divorce, high levels of consistent narcissistic gaslighting, abuse, bullying, solo parenting, working, juggling and wearing multiple hats on any given day. It virtually destroyed me on a deep soul level. And I LIVED in that energy for an extensive period of time. It was the perfect storm brewing, in conjunction with other random pieces of the puzzle previously playing out in the background.

As for food, I am not perfect. I am human. I have cravings here and there. I eat chocolate, just not the brands most of the population would be consuming. I have cravings for crunchy peanut butter. Again, simply a cleaner version to most of the brand names on the supermarket shelves. I snack randomly when there's elevated emotions or I'm watching a movie, or if it is cold or raining outside. My weight fluctuates slightly here and there and, of course, I am a woman - so occasionally, elevated HORMONES!

However, anything I am consuming NOW is my choice to do so – with full awareness of what it is, what is in it and what the consequences will be if I over-indulge. I am a big believer in the 80/20 rule when it comes to lifestyle. If 80% is positive and healthy then by all means, go enjoy yourself the other 20% of the time. Life is for LIVING.

Although, for me personally, nothing compares to just how good healthy FEELS.
And now even more so.

I ceased drinking alcohol and coffee for the first 9 months of my healing journey. I initially believed it would be rather challenging and was waiting for my brain to go into meltdown. However, truth be told, I breezed through it. Granted, I was only a minimal coffee drinker – and social drinker. I realised the majority of the time that these things are simply a habit, or familiar routine, mostly performed on autopilot, essentially becoming a crutch to lean on when we've had a good day, a bad day or have a big day ahead of us! Usually, as is the case with coffee, the very first task most people undertake when they head into the kitchen in the morning, is switch the kettle or coffee machine on, or line up at the coffee shop, with virtually nothing else happening until they get their "fix".

It's a habit. It's a learned behaviour. We weren't born drinking coffee. Therefore, if we never had it, we would never miss it. And don't get me wrong, I love a great coffee! However, there is the addictive component to caffeine, and the acidity level (usually around 5pH), as is most alcohol. Again, it showed me what mindset can do. When we truly, honestly make the decision, no matter what it is, and ANCHOR it into our minds and our core, we can do ANYTHING. We aren't born with a latte in our hands or a cold beer or wine. These become CHOICES as we grow up. It's a social connection and has become a part of many cultures. At the core of it all, we know too much of either isn't healthy or great for our body. But what about the energetic component to these and the foods we consume?

Everything is energy. What we are consuming is VITAL to our own life force. They are either helping or hindering the path to complete wellness. Treating your body like a garbage disposal is not going to do your weight, your energy levels, your clarity of mind, your organs or your mood any favours. Consuming junk food regularly actually has the same effect on your liver (the body's largest detoxifier) as drinking alcoholic beverages. You may not see the effects straight away, but believe me when I say:

You cannot cheat your body. It's keeping a record, either internally or externally - or both - of everything you consume.

Processed, canned and GMO foods are described as "dead" foods or dead energy and are so highly processed there is nothing "living" about them. Coffee and alcohol are also low vibrational.

· ·

"The food you eat can be either the safest and most powerful form of medicine or the slowest form of poison." – Ann Wigmore

· ·

In David Hawkins book, Power vs Force, regular coffee resonates at 223 (lower end of frequency scale) out of 1000 (highest vibration). Whilst it isn't the worst, it's also not the best and still very low on the frequency scale. And whilst there are a multitude of different alcoholic drinks, wine for example resonates around 250. And alcohol in general, can take up to 10 days (even I did not know this!) for the body to recalibrate to the vibration level it was at before it was consumed.

A happy person can typically have a drink or two and their vibration can stay quite high afterwards, as this is their predominant state of being. Yet a person who has a generally negative outlook on life, or is going through something life-changing like a loss, can sink deeper into the funk of depression, low mood, sadness and anxiety. Their vibration will continue to decrease.

Furthermore, alcohol can, (depending on your mood and vibration at the time), open your body up to psychic attacks, dark energy attachments and "spirits".

Sugary foods and drinks for instance, can create holes or fractures in your aura, allowing denser energies to penetrate, throwing your chakras out of balance and interfering with your spiritual and physical progress in general.

Most of us understand that gratitude, truth and love have the highest energy vibrations. But most do not even think of, or understand, that the food we CONSUME also holds high and low frequencies.
The vibration of food is fundamentally derived from the energy it was created with – and made with. That is, the energy and intention that is put into, and absorbed by the food whilst it is also grown, produced or even being physically prepared.

If you are in an angry mood for example, you're pissed off at the world, at work, your partner, whatever it is, then regardless of whether you are the one preparing it or eating it, that anger vibration is also directed into the meal you are preparing or eating. You literally CONSUME the vibration of anger when you sit down to eat it. This might be somewhat challenging to grasp initially, but I am sure there have been times you can remember eating when angry, frustrated, arguing, crying, depressed and the act of eating that meal at the time wasn't really that enjoyable. Yes, of course it is predominantly the emotional state at play in that moment, but energy T-R-A-N-S-F-E-R-S.

Unconscious eating is one of the primary causes of digestive and hormonal issues and your body's ability to assimilate food correctly and efficiently.

There is a reason REAL LIVING food has a high vibe and choosing to eat this way will also raise your own frequency. The highest frequency foods are those grown organically, grown locally and in season. These are **not** grown with pesticides, herbicides, not genetically modified and have a higher mineral content due to the quality of soil they are grown in. This is another reason that local farmers markets are gaining more and more popularity!

The most important step in shifting to a higher vibrational diet is to be patient and kind to yourself. It probably won't happen overnight but by gradually crowding out some of the less than healthy options you may have chosen in the past, with more "living" foods, you will begin to look and FEEL better! And feeling is a powerful state of BE-ing. How we FEEL is ultimately how we will BE.

No matter what adversity you are currently facing in your life, what you are consuming, on all levels, but especially what you eat, will be fundamental in keeping not only your physical body in an optimum state, but also keeping your mental state clean and clear and better equipped to handle what life is throwing at you.

Keeping your body and mind functioning at optimal levels is a crucial part of facing an adversity or crisis, but also crucial to HEALING from any health challenge.

Green foods, think broccoli, spinach, chard, broccolini, kale, especially organic, are some of THE highest vibrational foods. Does it mean that everyone can eat them? No! There are so many variables when it comes to food and nutrition, that's why there are so many eating lifestyles out there. We are all different. Different ages, different gut health issues, different blood types, different ethnic backgrounds, different jobs with different hours, different locations around the world, different health challenges and of course, different DNA. The bottom line is – healthy food will help you achieve not only a healthy body, but also a healthy, clear mind.

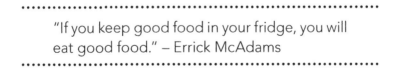

"If you keep good food in your fridge, you will eat good food." – Errick McAdams

That's why, as with medicine, there isn't just ONE way. You must find what works for YOU. And it could be a mix of a few different modalities. What resonates with your body, your lifestyle, your commitment and your desire to WANT to be healthier and thrive - not just get by and survive.

Additionally, mindful eating is another important part of the equation. When was the last time you truly paid attention to what you were eating WHILE you were eating it? This is a big red flag for me, especially as a solo parent. In fact, I'm sure most parents can relate to this one. We are so busy multi-tasking that breakfasts, lunches and dinner times can often feel like we are literally eating standing up or on the go.

Years of clock watching in the mornings to execute school runs, work appointments or catching flights did not always leave adequate time to sit and focus on fueling my body correctly. Practising the fine art of being present at mealtimes whilst consciously digesting our food, rather than carelessly wolfing it down, is vitally important. Bad habits such as standing whilst eating or mindlessly eating will often leave our body feeling empty afterwards as the brain-gut connection is not linked in harmony and will completely disassociate any amount of food you may have already consumed.

Balance is key. Knowing, not ignoring the signs your body is giving you every single day. Your body is an amazing machine that very few of us give thanks for. Think about the number of functions and movements it performs for you. EVERY. SINGLE. DAY.

One of the simplest ways to reconnect is to silently and consciously ASK your body what it needs because we are all so different. As I mentioned earlier, what works for one may not be suitable for another. You know YOU.

More importantly, vibrationally, how do you want your body to FEEL?

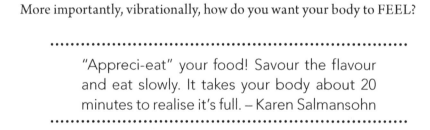

"Appreci-eat" your food! Savour the flavour and eat slowly. It takes your body about 20 minutes to realise it's full. – Karen Salmansohn

I highly recommend buying certified organic where possible to reduce the pesticides and chemicals and allow your body to absorb the highest vibrational food possible. Bear in mind, not all produce has to be organic. For those on a budget or with a family, I often direct people to the Environmental

Working Group website. Every year they release what is called "The Dirty Dozen" and "The Clean Fifteen".

Pending growing your own fruits and vegetables, the Dirty Dozen list is essentially the top twelve most highly sprayed fruits and vegetables to avoid buying (where possible) unless organic. If that is not viable, then rinse your produce with a specific fruit and vegetable wash that is easily sourced online or from your local health food store. Alternatively, simply soaking your produce in the kitchen sink and adding a couple of capfuls of good old apple cider vinegar, then rinsing and drying will remove any pesticides and herbicides. Another great invention are portable ionisers that can be placed in a sink with your produce, lifting the chemical residue off safely and leaving your fruit and vegetables fresh and clean.

The Clean Fifteen are the top 15 fruits and vegetables that DO NOT need to be organic as they are least likely to be affected by chemicals and sprays i.e bananas – as you peel the skin off to eat therefore the actual fruit itself is protected from absorbing the chemicals and sprays.
The bottom line with food is to ensure you are eating as close to the food source as possible, organic where viable, with the least amount of processing, packaging and added ingredients.

Below is a short, generalised list of where most foods sit in frequency levels. Of course, it is impossible to name every food source, however this is a quick reference and simplified list. Organic INCREASES the frequency of any food you are consuming, especially for selected fruits and vegetables.

SUPER HIGH FREQUENCY (very high life force energy) 52MHz – 320MHz
Premium quality essential oils, chlorophyll, wheatgrass, spirulina, phytoplankton

HIGH FREQUENCY FOODS: 15MHz
Raw, fresh fruits and vegetables
Seaweed
Raw chocolate
Cold-pressed freshly squeezed juices
Sprouts like alfalfa, watercress

Certain grains like amaranth, brown rice, buckwheat, oats,
Legumes, nuts and seeds, fermented foods
Herbs and spices

MEDIUM FREQUENCY FOODS: 5MHz
Lightly steamed or stir-fried fresh vegetables
Potatoes and wheat (pasta) – when boiled correctly, are the only two exceptions
Sun-dried or properly dehydrated fruits
Raw honey
Raw cacao
Olive oil, peanut oil, avocado oil, coconut oil

LOW FREQUENCY FOODS: 0Mhz
Standard tea, coffee
(very heavily sprayed - coffee is one of THE most chemically treated crops + tea bags are predominantly bleached in chlorine that you then add hot water to and drink)
Commercial chocolate, sweets, lollies
Deep-fried foods
(higher risks of obesity, heart disease, type 2 diabetes and cancer)
Most cheeses – dairy in general
(highly inflammatory and mucus forming in the body)

FOODS THAT LOWER YOUR VIBRATION: The following foods are those that are most negative (dead energy) to the body when consumed. Unfortunately, virtually ALL meat from animals is dead energy as it rots and ferments in the body over time. There are significantly higher rates of various cancers such as bowel and colon cancers in those who consume large amounts of red meat, and in particular processed meats from the deli, sausages, ham, hotdogs, salami, smoked meats and jerky.

Additionally, other contributing factors include the food the animals have been given, (think large scale GMO feedlots, antibiotics, vaccines and more), as this is passed through to the meat, as well as the way in which they are destroyed, with high levels of cortisol, fear and shock pumping through their veins prior to their demise. I haven't personally eaten red meat for many years and choose to consume mainly fish, organic/free range chicken on occasion or vegan. I highly recommend giving up meat or reducing your consumption to perhaps 1-2 weekly and invest in organic, pasture-fed and raised animal products.

Conventional packaged foods are also ones to be avoided, as these are usually loaded in preservatives, numbers, additives, flavours and flavour enhancers like MSG – basically anything but natural, let alone high frequency. Every time you consume these products, you are essentially cancelling out any energy work you may be doing, and this can set you back by days, weeks or even months if they make up a predominant part of your nutritional intake.

Avoid or strictly limit these foods if spiritual growth and high vibrational living is a priority for you.

- Margarine / Pasteurised milk
- Cooked sausages and meats of any description – dead flesh
- Alcoholic drinks / Refined sugars
- Bleached flours
- GMO foods / Processed foods
- Ready-to-eat basic meals like frozen pizzas, soups, etc.
- Conventional canned vegetables and fruits
- Foods that contain preservatives, hydrogenated fats, artificial flavours and colours
- Virtually anything with a long shelf life

I will reiterate this once more - you cannot cheat your body.

> "By cleansing your body on a regular basis and eliminating as many toxins as possible from your environment, your body can begin to heal itself, prevent disease, and become stronger and more resilient than you ever dreamed possible!" – Dr. Edward

SUMMARY OF MY DAILY EATING PLAN:

I will highlight that my eating style is simple, clean and as close to the natural source as possible. In other words, predominantly unprocessed foods. I have only myself and Chanel to prepare for, and thankfully she eats very closely to myself, so our mealtimes are kept simple, yet healthy and fresh. So, for the greater majority of households of four or more, there are literally thousands of healthy meal plans online for whatever budget and numbers you are prepping for, recipes, specific meals for specific health issues, blood types and much more.

Perhaps research the areas you require help or inspiration with when it comes to eating clean and high vibe, along with sourcing different options and recipes formulated to work for YOU and YOUR FAMILY. If you need extra motivation or support, then I highly encourage you to work with a holistic health coach or integrative wellness coach to help get you started. Overall, 90-95% of the foods, condiments, cooking oils and supplements mentioned below are ORGANIC. In between, I consumed nothing but Alka Power water and organic roasted dandelion tea.

Yes, there were days in the latter phase of my journey where I deviated or succumbed to a few unaccounted handfuls of organic corn chips or a few extra pieces of dark organic 70%+ cacao chocolate. Sometimes I had more than a few. Just not the whole bag or the whole block. Big difference.

The reality is, the cleaner you are eating, the less cravings you will likely have. As an A blood type, I've never craved pizza, pasta or other heavy, high carb dishes but I do enjoy them occasionally. This does not mean don't eat them. On the contrary, you can still enjoy a significant portion of your favourite things when you understand HOW to swap out or replace conventional ingredients for cleaner options.

In full disclosure, my biggest craving was (clean/organic) crunchy peanut butter! Spoonfuls of it - especially on days I didn't feel like eating or was simply lacking time or motivation. Probably not the best choice but it was what my body wanted.

So I did.

UPON RISING: 20ml x fulvic humic liquid with 10 x MSM drops or 1 teaspoon of MSM powder, 1 x high strength zinc, 1 x berberine, 1 x magnesium tablet or 4-5 pumps of magnesium spray on the body, 1 x 32 million (10 strains) probiotic
6 x Braftovi + 3 x Mektovi

+ B-epic power green Elev8, 2 x black seed oil capsules, 1 x tablespoon liposomal C + D3
(these was incorporated back in after about 9 months)

*BREAKFAST (when I wasn't fasting): 2-3 x eggs, rye or low carb toast, smashed avocado, yeast flakes, olive oil, himalayan salt
* 3 x Mektovi + 6 x Braftovi

11am – 6-8 x IP-6+inositol + 1 x berberine

LUNCH: *When I was fasting, I simply ate breakfast at lunchtime.
VEGGIE BLENDS JUICE – carrot, celery, beetroot and ginger OR carrot, turmeric, orange, apple, lemon/lime or dandelion tea

When I felt like something sweet - Coconut yoghurt or organic oats w/ blueberries, shredded coconut, pumpkin seeds, chia seeds, brazil nuts or almonds (for a bit of crunch), cacao nibs (who doesn't want a chocolate fix but the healthy version!), vegan vanilla protein powder

OR:

Low carb sunflower and linseed bun with avocado, tomato, cucumber, hummus, mixed leafy greens, Himalayan salt/pepper ADD chicken if I felt like it + organic dandelion tea

DINNER: VEGGIE BLEND: organic steamed greens (various combinations of spinach, kale, asparagus, broccoli/broccolini, bok choy, cauliflower, avocado, zucchini, mushrooms, pumpkin seeds, walnuts or brazil nuts, olive oil, yeast flakes (great substitute for cheese and very high in B vitamins), garlic, Braggs mixed herbs/spices, Himalayan salt

SALAD BLEND: mixed leafy salad greens, cherry tomatoes, cucumber, avocado, mushrooms, carrot, pumpkin seeds, brazil nuts/walnuts, goats fetta (when I felt like "cheese"), and through spring and summer added mango/watermelon/apple/strawberries (whatever was in season), olive oil, apple cider vinegar, balsamic, yeast flakes, Himalayan salt

PROTEIN: either grilled chicken breast, tuna or tuna steak, or brown rice/veggie/lentil burger or grilled salmon or snapper fillet - or I would make an omelette
*3 x Mektovi with dinner

SNACKS: Organic dark (70-85% +) chocolate or
Few teaspoons of crunchy peanut butter (organic and 100% nuts)

BEFORE BED: 5ml x cannabis oil + THC

B-epic detox + B-epic sleep
(these were incorporated back in after about 9 months)
More information on the B-Epics can be found through my personal link

B-EPIC | Add More Life to Your Years (bepic.com)

> "From the bitterness of disease man learns the sweetness of health." – Catalan Proverb

MIRACLE INSPIRATION: Stop and smell the roses. Take time each day to connect with your body. Are you feeding it dead food with dead energy or are you feeding it whole, living, vibrant foods, that have you not only surviving, but thriving?

Take note of your environment and your energy when you are preparing or eating your food. Slow down and prepare and eat with LOVE and gratitude.

Note to self!

....

"Sorry, there's no magic bullet. You gotta eat healthy and live healthy to be healthy and look healthy. End of story." — Morgan Spurlock

....

Chapter 16

MINDFUL MOVEMENT - Healing your body through physical activity and the magical powers of grounding in nature

....

"Physical fitness is not only one of the most important keys to a healthy body, it is the basis of dynamic and creative intellectual activity." – John F. Kennedy

....

How you treat your body is how it will treat YOU.

This doesn't only apply to food.

Throughout this book, I have talked about the importance of mindset, energy work, vibration, food and frequencies and now physical movement and grounding in nature, when it comes to health and healing, either physically, emotionally or both.

Our bodies are designed to MOVE.

Period.

Yet our sedentary lifestyles are virtually dominating our current daily routines. Sitting is essentially becoming the new smoking, and as such, is creating an entire set of new, yet serious health issues. Believe me when I say, if you are facing ANY crisis, unless you are physically unable to move, there should be a priority on small actionable steps (figuratively and literally) to moving your body frequently – with intention - at least 3-4 times a week, if not daily. Exercise POSITIVELY affects not only our physical state but also our mental and emotional state.

Amid life's challenges, a shocking diagnosis or a deep loss or adversity, one of the most important things you can continue to do is move your body. Why? Because it has an amazing effect on your mindset, lowers depression and anxiety, usually gives you MORE energy afterwards, especially if it becomes a regular routine, leaves you FEELING better, more able to cope under stressful or intense situations, increases lymphatic flow and circulation, helps lubricate the joints like oil in a car motor and is one of THE main channels for releasing toxins, opening up your detoxification pathways via the lymphatic system, as well as through sweating.

Does this mean you have to be a gym junkie? Absolutely not.
Find what works for YOU.
For your routine.
Find what works around your schedules.
Your commitments.
Your family.
Your current flexibility and mobility.
Your timeframes.
Just don't find an excuse.

Walking, for example, is the simplest and most underestimated whole body exercise a person can do. It requires zero gym memberships, no equipment, can be done pretty much anywhere, conditions the entire body, works the heart and lungs and is also low impact for those with joint issues.

Walking is just an example. It truly doesn't matter what form of movement you choose if it's done regularly throughout the week and is something you can COMMIT to and most of all, ENJOY doing! From an emotional standpoint, it is also exercising the mind, sending blood flow and oxygen to the brain that in turn leads to greater clarity, an increase in focus and triggering endorphins to assist you in feeling better overall. Through adversity and general shitty times, feeling physically healthy is a very important goal and one that shouldn't be overlooked or dismissed.

We are all so uniquely different. Therefore, in addition to food, our choice or ability level when it comes to exercise is also heavily influenced by our different ages, different hobbies, different likes, dislikes, different physical limitations, locations and so on.

Movement also increases coordination, balance and stability.

It's a cliché but as I emphasised earlier, **find what works for you**. There's a reason you have probably heard that a thousand times. Because it's true! It could be gardening, dancing, golf, swimming (another great low impact exercise), cycling, yoga and more. Mixing it up is even more beneficial as you want to incorporate activities that work on flexibility, balance, endurance and strength.

When you find activities that you LOVE to do, they don't become a chore, or something forced, or unachievable. Instead, they become something you look forward to, activities that inspire you to try harder, do better, suit your level of fitness and bring you JOY.

An added bonus would be finding a friend, partner, support person or social gym pal to keep you company and join you along the way, because when it comes to creating new habits, or restarting after a period of time out, MOTIVATION and ACCOUNTABILITY is crucial to building and solidifying a healthier and more active lifestyle.

For me personally, I love being in the gym on my own, even though I am surrounded by many other like-minded individuals. I feel I am receiving the best of both worlds. Funnily enough, despite the fact most days are busy when I arrive, the gym is my quiet time, my think time, my decompression time, my vent time, my feel good time. Whether I show up and simply go through the motions, walk on the treadmill or find my strength for a weight session, whatever I am feeling, I am there to either build on it by feeling better, or shift it if I am feeling emotional, tired, stressed, in a low mood or frustrated. Regardless, I never walk out regretting that I walked in.

There were many days in the beginning, especially after the radiation, that I could've easily reneged on attending, however keeping my routine as normal as possible was a very important part in my healing process. There were countless times I would simply walk on the treadmill for an hour because that's all my body felt it could manage at the time.

Every day I showed up, regardless of what I did, I classed it as a WIN. I had every excuse to justify not being there, however I kept myself accountable and made it a non-negotiable. Keeping my mind strong was paramount, keeping my daily routine as normal as possible, and keeping my body MOVING, even if it was more slowly and carefully, was the best medicine for my SOUL.

On other occasions whilst walking on the beach, I would call close friends or family for moral support, particularly if my head was hurting, heavy, off balance or to simply elevate my mood if I was feeling low. Most importantly, this was incredibly healing for my body to connect with Mother Nature, soak up the sun's warmth, breathe fresh air, and feel revitalised and refreshed from the salt water on my feet.
Mentally, emotionally and physically.
Even if it was incremental.
One small but strategic step at a time.

I read my body well. Never taking it to extremes, yet intuitively knowing the positive flow on effects if I endured, regardless of whether it began that way. I often say to people - just START. One foot in front of the other. You will find the momentum to keep going as you move. The more you move the better you feel. The better you feel the more you persist and push forward.

I took advantage of every opportunity to listen to motivational or inspirational videos, my favourite music or podcasts. Even now in the gym, I transcend into my own little bubble whilst being surrounded and motivated by others. Alone mentally but not alone physically. It is definitely my happy place outside of the beach or just generally being in nature.

Every day is different, however I have deep appreciation for my body. More so now than ever before.

In addition, I have fallen in love with a selection of fast 5–15 minute home workout routines requiring zero equipment and using body weight only. Simply add ankle weights, resistance bands or use lighter hand held weights to take it to the next level. There are hundreds of short, sharp workouts on YouTube for specific body parts, based on a timeframe that suits and all done in the comfort and privacy of your own home. These are perfect if you have small children, are limited physically, work long hours, travel frequently or simply need some fresh routines and inspired motivation.
Zero gym required.

Ladies, some of my favourite channels are Lilly Sabri, Holly Dolke, Rebecca Louise, Bailey Brown and Eylem Abaci.

....

"It is exercise alone that supports the spirits and keeps the mind in vigour." – Marcus Tullius Cicero

....

Throughout this entire process, I have learnt to listen to my body more than ever before. Yes, there is a difference between pushing, and forcing your body to do what it simply does not want to do, or is too tired to do, and challenging your body and building strength.

During stressful times, your body should be treated like your best friend. Because it is. Your body is with you all day, every single day. And it's the only one you've got. Treat it with care, compassion and kindness on those days it doesn't perform like the circus monkey you think it should. And whilst movement is important, so is the self-care we show it in our downtime. Show some body love by going for a massage, making your favourite cup of tea, a pedicure, a facial, a nap, catching up with a friend for a laugh, watching a great movie, hot sauna or whatever floats your boat and makes you and your body feel good. I am speaking predominantly to the ladies here, but fellas you get my drift.

Over the years, for example, I have witnessed many women in (and outside of) the gym almost punishing themselves for the big night out, the girls weekend, the relationship breakup, trying to look like the latest Instagram or social media influencer, to _____ (fill in the blank), as though it's the end of the world or a dangerous form of body obsession. I know. In my twenties and thirties I would often do this too. Those feelings of guilt or remorse from over-indulging after a big night or social event or trying to measure up to some celebrity ideal that is physically impossible or predominantly airbrushed and photoshopped.

PUSHING, and PUNISHING the body to match up to unrealistic expectations. You might be exercising to extremes to physically or emotionally "work it off", or match society's standards, but that isn't exactly healthy. And your body knows it. So does your mind, and every single cell that you are sending those vibes into. Usually, a proportion of these extremes will emotionally stem from a lack of self-love, diminished self-worth and not feeling good enough.

"Movement should not be punishment."

Say thank you to your body every single day! Do you know just how incredibly amazing the human body is? Stop for a moment and take note of ALL the actions your body performs 24 hours a day on autopilot. Your fingers, toes, arms, legs, walking, bending, lifting, driving, picking up children, whatever your work entails physically, the organs keeping you alive and running your body equivalent to the motor in your car. But most importantly, your BREATH. Numerous body parts perform multiple functions simultaneously that we simply take for granted - until a minor mishap or major misfortune occurs, and the very basics of your body's movement is challenged, restricted, or completely stripped away from you.

Because everything is a blessing. No matter what state your body is in right now, start APPRECIATING it. Respecting it. Loving it. Begin talking to your body and praising it for carrying you throughout your day and performing the gazillion tasks required to get you out of bed in the mornings, to completing your work or daily checklists. Then finish the day by saying thank you before bedtime, as your body continues to function, heal, regenerate, rejuvenate and tune up while you sleep in order to repeat it all again tomorrow!

Purposeful physical movement is only going to AMPLIFY your energy, ACCELERATE your healing and ASSIST your body to eliminate and detoxify the vast amount of stored waste and cellular toxins, move the lymphatics and help release these via the skin and out through the bathroom.

There are multiple health hacks, especially for busy working professionals to incorporate more movement into your day. Probably the most recognised tip is taking the stairs, not the escalators. If possible, walk while you talk on the phone, even if it is around your office or home. If you sit at a desk, set an alarm every hour to remind yourself to get up and get moving. For every hour we sit, we are meant to move for a MINIMUM of ten minutes. Schedule walking meetings where possible. Park further away from your destination. Keep your sneakers in the car or leave a spare pair at the office and take advantage of lunch breaks if the weather is suitable.

For those at home, there is gardening, cleaning, walking the dog, doing short bouts of exercise during commercials, taking the kids to the park with a ball and more. Instead of online shopping, physically go to the stores instead if you can. Get creative.

And if you, or someone you know has been diagnosed with cancer, then exercise and activity should absolutely be part of your healing protocol as it will support your body in multiple ways. Where possible, combined with moderate resistance training, exercise can improve your response to treatments, improve mood and mental wellbeing (which is vitally important), helps alleviate fatigue, improves overall physical function, increases endurance, circulation, oxygen levels in the body and even reduces the likelihood of it recurring in other parts of the body.

Research has also shown that exercise is in fact a secret weapon in dealing with, and healing from cancer. Whilst researchers aren't exactly certain *how* it does what it does, they have found that exercise seems to pull senescent T-cells (essentially worn out immune cells) out into the bloodstream and marks them for death and disposal in the body, which in turn allows the body to then produce more killer T-cells that can fight off the cancer.

I feel this is one of the major factors in why I not only survived but continued to THRIVE throughout this entire journey. I maintained a high level of movement, gym and moderate resistance training virtually the entire time. Understandably not everyone may be able to do this, but if possible, just do SOMETHING. Listen to your body - and COMMIT.

Essentially, when talking to people in general about wellness, I often refer to our bodies like a car. We would never buy a car and not drive it right? Otherwise it would simply sit in the garage and eventually seize up or rust. Ultimately, the more we sit and sustain a sedentary lifestyle, the more likely our bodies will begin to seize up too.

Movement is like the oil in the car motor. It helps to circulate and increase blood flow, move the lymphatics, warm up the muscles, free up the joints, sends oxygen to the brain and into blood cells, increases flexibility and mobility, reduces stiffness and pain and improves sleep. Increasing your movement increases your overall health on so many levels!

Likewise, as with the car, when something is in need of repair, or not working efficiently, our bodies usually signal there is a problem or malfunction, similar to the oil light or the fuel light on the dashboard. Yet unlike the car, where we would promptly book it into a mechanic, check the oil or fill it up with fuel, many will continue to drive their bodies into the ground until eventually they break down and need more serious attention.

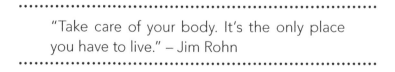

"Take care of your body. It's the only place you have to live." – Jim Rohn

Remember also, the major benefits of being outside, grounding in nature and how vitally important this is for your body's health and wellbeing. We have approximately 50 000 receptors underneath our feet that are designed to be "plugged in" to Mother Earth. Yet most of society in this day and age, are predominantly plugged into electronic devices emitting harmful EMF's, usually inside, sitting for long hours in front of screens or at desks, in cars, buses, trains and other forms of public transport. Sadly, society in general, is becoming sicker, despite the advancements in modern medicine. Illnesses, diseases and chronic health issues are continuously and disturbingly, on the rise.

> "Get yourself grounded and you can navigate even the stormiest roads in peace." — Steve Goodier

Many inflammatory diseases can be helped through grounding your body, and I mean barefoot, NO SHOES - on the grass, the dirt, the backyard, the beach, the ocean, in the park – anywhere your feet are physically touching the earth. Not only are you outside, (usually moving your body at the same time, so double wins!), this is powerful, as the earth carries electrons that literally re-energises all the cells in the body like a rechargeable battery, reduces pain, promotes better sleep, regulates cortisol levels, protects your body from harmful EMFs and of course, recalibrates and promotes HEALING in your body.

> "It is my conclusion that the human mind and body is essentially a single cell rechargeable battery that is charged from the atmospheric DC voltage and the Earth." — Steven Magee

This is a very short list of benefits, so I encourage you to research this further and most importantly, to EXPERIENCE the difference for yourself by implementing it regularly. We feel so much better when we have been outside in nature. Seasons and different parts of the world will of course play a role; however it is literally akin to having a free tune up and a session of reflexology all rolled into one!

Being brought up on a farm, I was barefoot at every opportunity. Even now, one of my favourite things to do is kick my shoes off when I can, and walk barefoot outside in nature in the fresh air and sunshine. Most western children will spend their entire day ungrounded – from the moment they wake up, to the moment they go to bed. They may be outside playing, however if they have shoes on, they are still disconnected from the earth. Of course, being outside is better than being inside! Proper grounding however, is absolutely VITAL to their health, and growth, as well as regulating their moods and sleep. And of course, every parent's dream - burning off energy through movement!

....

"Most children have been cursed with parents who have forgotten the joy of walking barefoot." — Mokokoma Mokhonoana

....

Now if for some reason this is impossible – snow, freezing cold, extreme heat, lack of time, environment is not optimal or safe – there is a multitude of earthing and grounding products available online that mimic the earth's natural charge, such as earthing shoes, chair pads, foot mats, car mats, pet beds, blankets, sheets, virtually anything you need for adults, children and pets, as well as insoles that are designed to reconnect the body to the earth.

Simply search "earthing products" and the country you are in and see where your intuition guides you.

I have also included a personal link to VIBESUP (vibrational energy products) that, over the years, I have purchased charging mats, crystals, EMF blockers and more through. Just one of many ethical companies I use and support, as they have an amazing reputation in the USA as well as worldwide, depending on what you are specifically seeking. So no excuses.

Vibrational Energy Education and Tools | VibesUP.com

> "When we feel the ground beneath our feet, the sun on our faces and the oxygen in our lungs, we experience the world around us and reconnect with nature." — Shawn Wells

Bottom line - schedule more time for physical movement, and preferably outside when the weather permits. Your body will thank you.

MIRACLE INSPIRATION: Your body was designed to MOVE!
The old saying, **if you don't move it, you lose it** is true.
Nothing changes if nothing changes.
Find what works for you.
Every day you choose.
Choosing to remain where you are physically or choosing to move your body more, in whatever form that takes and whatever capacity that may be, based on YOUR personal circumstances and health.

Find time to ground in nature - barefoot. Even if it means finding a patch of grass and standing or sitting still while your feet connect to the Earth.

Remember to take a moment every day to APPRECIATE your body.
Bottom line – LOVE IT HARD.

> "Doctors won't make you healthy. Nutritionists won't make you slim. Teachers won't make you smart. Gurus won't make you calm. Mentors won't make you rich. Trainers won't make you fit.
> Ultimately, you have to take responsibility.
> Save yourself."
> – Naval Ravikant

Chapter 17

RECOVERY ROAD – Life is a marathon, not a sprint. Adjust your speed accordingly and to the conditions.

••

"When you walk into the presence of people who calibrate at the very highest energy levels, just being in their energy field, everything that is dis-eased or in dis-harmony is healed. When you bring a higher and a more loving energy to the presence of disorder or disharmony or disease, you are really bringing a healing energy.

And that's what healing is involved with: It's no longer allowing yourself to wallow around in a process in which you tell yourself that you don't have the capacity to be able to transcend whatever it is that's bothering you or hurting you or killing you." - Wayne Dyer

••

The race is not given to the swift but those who can endure to the end.
The same applies to healing.

I'm sure you've experienced a time when driving, where you've had cars zip past you, radically weaving in and out of lanes, only to watch as they sped off into the distance. I certainly have. On numerous occasions. Maybe you have even been that person. At the time I generally presume they are in a mad hurry to reach their destination, are late for work or a scheduled appointment, or they're clearly being incredibly reckless.

Ironically, and in addition to that, have you then found yourself somehow beside them at the next set of lights or further down the highway in a traffic jam?

All that expended energy and HAST did not actually get them anywhere you weren't going in the bigger scheme of things. Moral of the story:

Speed does not always equal PROGRESS.

There will come a time when this statement will ring true for you.
Amidst life's challenges, don't try to rush to the finish line.
Whatever that is for you right now.

Perhaps it feels like those around you are accomplishing more, doing more, are in front of you in finances, career, love, homes, cars, material things, and on the outside that may be true. Sometimes however, it is in the slowness and steadiness of your own journey where you will discover those big, priceless nuggets of gold about YOURSELF.

It might be your patience and ability to stay calm under pressure, your ability to focus regardless of distractions, your endurance to stay the course or your navigational skills in manoeuvring through uncertain situations.

Even when those around you have their proverbial foot on the gas and seem to be racing off into the distance to collect their next big thing at warp speed.

In those moments, from the driver's seat, it appears you have been left in the dust feeling as though they will surely arrive at their destination well before you, if you ever arrive at all.

Nothing will kill your enthusiasm, your drive, your inspiration and hope faster than comparison syndrome.

Stay in your own lane.
Even if it feels ridiculously SLOW.
Or has stalled completely.
Pace yourself.
Breathe.
Everything is happening exactly as it should be and in Divine perfect timing. You are always in the right place at the right time. Especially when it doesn't look like it or feel like it. Get comfortable with being UNCOMFORTABLE.

You will arrive at your destination at the perfect time.

The same applies to healing - on all levels. Mind, body and spirit.
We are all on our own individual paths, so in reality there is no race. The only race is in your mind. Noone is beating you.
At anything.
Their GPS is simply set on an entirely different destination with its own detours, delays, proverbial flat tyres, breakdowns, accidents, trade ins and upgrades. All you can see from the outside right now is their season of upgrades. The good stuff.
Yours is coming.

Yes, there is free will. If you travel too far in the wrong direction, take a corner too fast or wind up at a dead end, the Divine Creator and universe will step in, and course correct to place you back on the right road. In reality this may feel like multiple tower moments or complete and utter upheaval. Things may quite literally be falling apart or falling down around you. TRUST anyway. Absolutely nothing that is happening in your life right now is a surprise to the Creator, no matter how disastrous, how heartbreaking or how insurmountable the challenge you may be facing.

Likewise, you cannot rush healing. REAL healing. Recovery road is a place we will all end up on at some point in our lives after at least one or two major upheavals, challenges, losses, adversities or illnesses.

Think of the times you had something as simple as a cold. You know it's not the end of the world. Every so often it may feel like it though, especially when you are smack bang in the middle of recovering. Your body feels heavy, exhausted, blocked up, aching. You know you will come out the other side but recovery is still needed and it's usually slow and steady, and in the moment it feels like forever! Yes, we can assist the body to heal faster but the reality is we can't skip steps and press fast forward.

There is always a purpose for the delays.
A message from the mess.
A testimony from the test.
Where you are right now is not where you will STAY.

You are most likely being positioned for something bigger and better. You just can't SEE it yet.
And just because you can't see anything happening, doesn't mean NOTHING is happening. Others may have written you off, just as the medical establishment and others did with me, but God does His best work in secret. Behind closed doors. In complete silence. And usually in the darkness and confusion. Otherwise, He wouldn't be God and it wouldn't be a miracle, right?

God doesn't need to have His proverbial ducks in a row to make magic and miracles happen. God created ducks and can make those ducks do whatever He wants when He wants. What I am trying to say here, is that at any moment, and probably when you least expect it, when you feel like things are so completely off-course, off-kilter and in complete chaos and you have travelled to the end of the road, that's when things usually change, a sudden shift happens, a way out appears and everything falls into place. When you have FAITH and TRUST and full unwavering BELIEF in the Creator, those ducks will line up so spectacularly at the designated set time, that everyone around you will have no other logical explanation than to say it was an absolute MIRACLE.

Never underestimate God's next BIG move.

Human psychology is to AVOID pain at all costs and get out of it at lightning speed. Unfortunately, that is usually not how the Divine works.

Throughout my journey I had many moments of reminding myself that God is in control. Even when it was a complete mess. Nothing was or ever will be a surprise to Him. So with that in mind, I was able to keep calm and stay anchored regardless of what was showing up in my reality, knowing that everything was exactly as it should be. Good or not so good at the time, and that everything would eventually be ok and work out, however long that took, and in whatever way that looked.

On the Tuesday following the MRI, I had my regular monthly hospital visit for the usual blood tests and standard chat with my oncologist. This day, however, was also the day I would find out the results from the PET/CT scans done on my body the week prior. Could I have phoned the hospital and found out verbally first? Most probably. But a little voice just said *"Don't worry about it. It is what it is. The results cannot be changed. It is already done. If it were negative, then the hospital would've called you by now."*

With that in mind, I stayed centred, calm, and grounded, regardless of the pending results – because that is exactly how God wanted it to be. As the morning rolled around, I spoke my gratitude list out loud while I dressed, had breakfast, and took Chanel to school. I kissed her goodbye and proceeded to the gym for my usual morning workout routine.
I remember listening to a few motivational YouTube channels whilst I was there to uplift me and keep my mindset focused on the outcome I was praying for, and desired so badly.

I drove to the hospital speaking to my guides and angels that whatever unfolded I would accept it and be ok with it. No matter what. Then I took some big, deep breaths.

I parked my car and headed into the Outpatients Oncology Ward. Little did I know it was going to be a long wait with a stream of people and multiple delays in appointments. This same day was a staff lunch I had to for-go, and wondered how everyone was, partly wishing I was there.

It would be nearly an hour and half later that my name would finally get called.

I was greeted outside the patient room by my familiar oncologist, whom I had nicknamed Dr Who, stemming from a rather funny marketing banner inside the ward with his face smack bang in the middle of other oncologists, similar to a reality TV show promotion. The catch phrase was in essence, a tongue-in-cheek play on words as to WHO will be your oncologist.

He smiled and ushered me into the room and began with the usual *"How are you? How are you feeling? How has everything been?"*
After my usual responses of *"I'm great thank you. I feel good. Everything has been fine."*
We got down to the nitty gritty.

"So I'm guessing the scans were ok? I figured you would've called me if they were bad?"

And with a little chuckle he replied, *"Yes yes. Your scans look good."*
We made small talk for a minute or two, whilst he brought them up on the computer screen for us both to view. Even though I was quickly becoming a professional at reading and deciphering medical images, I asked him to explain them in more detail for me.

He proceeded to firstly enlarge my lungs, which to me still visually appeared to have marks on them, but I was to discover that the main melanoma cluster had all but disappeared! It was nothing more than a very small mark, almost like a tiny money spider, where once it had been very pronounced, quite large and obviously far from ideal. He explained to me that this was just scarring, very common and nothing to worry about and could quite possibly continue to show up on future scans. Winning!

Dr Who then enquired about the latest MRI performed privately only a week earlier and so I brought up the brain scans on my phone to show him. Now remember, I had previously attended my brief appointment with Jim, receiving virtually zero explanation or feedback, other than the immunotherapy conversation. In that short space of time, he printed off the report, wrote another MRI referral and explained that my brain was looking good.

Outside of that, I had assumed it was tracking in the right direction and let it go.

On this day however, Dr Who decided he would closely investigate and observe the scans. We chatted about how good things were looking, he enlarged pictures of the brain and explained what I was looking for, and in the body. With each image came further positive statements. I felt a sudden urge to speak intuitively.

"What are you trying to tell me here?"

And his response shocked me.
He said, *"Well I guess you are what we would call in remission."*
I responded almost stunned, *"What?? As in I have no cancer left in my body?"*

He replied, *"Well yes and no. Everything here, even though there are still some inactive lesions in the brain and the small marker on the lung, they are all inactive, shrinking or stable or have completely disappeared and there is absolutely no growth or activity detected at all."*

The smile on my face no doubt lit up the entire room! Of course, he turned to me and said, *"Just remember that melanoma cells can hide and lie dormant in the body so yes, whilst we would technically class you as in remission, it is early days yet."*

"Yes, yes, I understand all of that. I know what I have been dealing with and I am well aware of what I was facing. So would you class this result as unusual?"

"Yes it is. Given where things were sitting in the beginning, obviously we can look after your body all day long, but it is the brain that was and is the main priority. But these results are definitely not what would be standard in an extreme case like yours. Just keep doing what you are doing."

"So, I guess my other protocols are working then?" I said cheekily with a grin on my face.

"Yes Kathy. But you could also say it was the medications too. You could perhaps give them some credit too." he said with a smile.

"Well of course I could, and I am very grateful. But I'll go with maybe a combination then."   -
We both had a laugh. Both respecting and acknowledging each other's point.

"So, what I will do is give you a week off the meds to build up your white blood cell count as the blood tests showed they had reduced again but this is a very common side effect. I will let your body have a rest and you can recommence them a week from today. I'll write you another script and I'll see you in 5 weeks from now, ok?"

After saying yes and thank you a few more times, I bounced out of his patient room all smiles and feeling amazing.

I cannot count how many times over the following days and week I quietly said thank you. Thank you to God, thank you to my soul team, thank you to my angels, thank you to my guides, thank you to Jay and Bianca, thank you to my work colleagues and thank you to family and friends.

In the lead up to this day I had been seeing the number 14 everywhere around me. At the time I kept thinking yes, I know 14 is one of my numbers. It's my birth date, Chanel's birth date, it's followed me everywhere on many occasions.
Significant life events have occured on the 14th.

That day however, in amongst the usual morning flurry to drop her to school I wasn't paying attention to dates. All I recalled was that it was Tuesday, a.k.a hospital appointment day. In all honesty, it wasn't until school pick up time that I was reminded again of the number 14, as the words, *"look at the date"* popped into my head.

Pulling out my phone, I swiped the screen to unlock it, and there it was:

Tuesday 14 September 2021.

Boom! Signs and synchronicities everywhere.

A flush of goosebumps covered my body as I gazed up to the sky smiling. After saying thank you under my breath a few more times, I noticed one of Chanel's little friends looking somewhat lost, so naturally enquired where her mum was. She rolled her eyes and said, *"probably running late as usual."* Her answer made me giggle, however I reassured her that regardless, we would wait around until her mum arrived. The girls ran off to play as I sat down on the oval embankment in the afternoon sunshine, feeling immense release, relief and gratitude.

About ten minutes later, I caught sight of her mother walking across the netball courts and stood up to greet her. After the usual hellos and thank you's for looking after her daughter she asked how I was. Now up until this point I had been VERY selective as to who knew my story, to protect not only my energy but to ensure Chanel's life was easier at school. At no point did I want teachers or students coming to her asking if her mum had cancer.

This particular afternoon however, we both sat down again in the sunshine to let the girls continue playing, and in that moment, I thought to myself, *"What the hell, just tell her."*

So I turned to her and simply said, *"I was diagnosed with incurable, inoperable stage 4 brain cancer in February and told I had 6 months to live. Today, instead of my time being up, I was given the news I am technically in remission."*

I'm sure her face fell open at the same time she responded, *"Oh wow! Oh my god I had no idea! OMG! That's amazing!"*

As I sat there and filled her in a little more, especially on the events leading up to this moment, and of having a benign mole removed from my back 4 years earlier, she turned to me and said," *You know, I had a scare when I was in my twenties. I went to the doctor, as I had a mole on my back that had changed colour, just like yours. It ticked all the boxes and they wanted me to have it removed as soon as possible. It was very raised and itchy, but it was late in the week when I got the news and I had already booked a girl's weekend away for a friend's birthday, so I told them I'd deal with it when I got back.*

I didn't want to ruin my weekend or my girlfriend's weekend. So, we went away, had an amazing time and came home late on Sunday evening. The strange thing was, the next day I woke up, proceeded to get dressed like any other workday, and all I could feel was this little indent in my back. When I looked in the mirror it was gone. It had literally fallen off! I went in for my follow up appointment that day and told my doctor. He checked my back and was shocked! He said in all the years of practising he had never seen that before. Everything was checked again where it had originally been, and I was given the all-clear. I'll never forget it. So ever since then I've been very careful and mindful, but I feel as though I was looked after by a higher power back then. You've really reminded me of all this today."

That conversation wasn't by chance.
Her initial story being similar to mine yet could've also gone in either direction. She then proceeded to tell me of another girlfriend who was going through treatment for breast cancer.
In my mind I was thinking, "*Wow, it's just everywhere, young and old, in some way, shape or form.*"

Spirit places people on your path to either help YOU - or for you to be of help to OTHERS. It could be an encouraging word, confirmation or a sign they were silently praying for, validation that they're on the right path or a piece of information that can assist them.

About five months later I was given a phone enquiry lead from work. It was early February 2022. As I began to chat to the gentleman, I asked him what health issues were troubling both him and his partner. I could not only hear, but also FEEL his voice change.

"*My wife has cancer.*"
I went silent.
In my mind I immediately thought, "*Another one.*"

I hesitated briefly, before intuitively feeling I needed to ask what type specifically. His response left me stunned and speechless.

"She has metastasized secondary brain cancer."
I nearly dropped the phone.
I thought to myself, *"Do I say anything or do I simply hold space for him to talk?"*
My intuition again nudged me, *"Do it."*
So, I told him briefly about my story.
He was shocked.
Our stories were almost a mirror of each other.

We spent the following 45 minutes talking about all of the things, diagnosis, treatments, tests, radiation and protocols.
I gave him as much information over the phone as I could without overloading and overwhelming him at the same time.
He was extremely grateful - and more importantly – HOPEFUL. I had given him HOPE that maybe, just maybe, there was a way out for his beautiful wife too.

In that sensitive and very raw moment, I realised that NONE of us should ever underestimate the power of HOPE, even if it is just a glimmer, when talking to people who are going through a challenge or major life event.
Sometimes all we need when facing insurmountable pain, heartbreak and sadness, is for someone to say, *"Hey, I see you. I hear you. You are not alone. I understand what you are going through. And it will be ok."*

I could hear his voice soften, and the fleeting moment of what sounded like quiet tears being shed. All he wanted was to see his beautiful wife, mother of his kids and his best friend to not be in pain, to be comfortable and hang on to that tiny thread of hope that maybe, just maybe, she could pull through too.

As I said goodbye and hung up the call, I knew once again that I was given that phone call on that day for that very reason.

Sometimes we will never know how deeply we touch or affect people's lives until AFTER we part ways. Since then, I have had many, many others reach out to me privately about family, friends or loved ones who are in the throes of dealing with cancer in some way, shape or form. All of them on their own recovery road, just wanting HOPE in the form of guidance, inspiration and answers.

Personally I look at life now like a movie, with an entire production crew directing the script. Different locations, different scenes, hundreds, if not thousands of extras, great story lines, plot twists, major losses, great joy and happiness, love, heartbreak, grief and more. So too, God is working behind the scenes right now, directing the right people to strategically show up for YOU in the right scene at the right time.

Some of them will be extras just filling in the background. Some will come in briefly only to return for another part later on. Others may have only one line, whilst some may appear from backstage and become centre stage in your life. Others will play the villains, the snakes in the grass or wolves in sheep's clothing, and some will play a starring role.

I walk through life with the complete understanding that we meet every single person for a reason, a lesson, a season or a lifetime. No matter how big or small, how heartbreaking or happy the part. Our souls have contracted to meet in those precise moments in this lifetime. It might take some time and some hardcore inner work but thank them all no matter what, positive or negative, no matter how difficult that may be.

If God has removed people, places and things from your life, just remember they were never part of your future, only passing through for a purpose and never meant to share in your shining moment centre stage.

∙∙∙

"My scars remind me that I did indeed survive my deepest wounds. That in itself is an accomplishment. And they bring to mind something else, too.

They remind me that the damage life has inflicted on me has, in many places, left me stronger and more resilient.

What hurt me in the past has actually made me better equipped to face the present." ~ Steve Goodie

••

MIRACLE INSPIRATION: There is a Higher Power.
Believe it. Know it. Trust it.
Anything is possible when it comes to Divine Intervention.

No matter where you are in this race called life.
No matter what you are up against.
No matter who has written you off.
No matter what you've lost or THINK you've lost.

When you have complete faith and trust in the Creator, He will make sure you cross YOUR finish line and claim your victory.
Every single time.

The key takeaway here is - it is YOUR race in this lifetime.
Your long drive.
Your marathon.
No one else's.
The course will be different.
The runners will be different.
The speed bumps. The detours. The wrong turns. The roundabouts. The dead ends. The breakdowns. The hills. The valleys. The mountains. The easy and effortless straight lines. The welcome and enjoyable down hill runs. All of it.
So cease comparing your GPS set destination with everyone else around you. Take the pressure off.
They aren't going where you are headed.

Every morning before I get out of bed, the first words out of my mouth are thank you for waking me up, thank you for this day, thank you for my breath and thank you for my healing.

God is my healer, my waymaker, my vindicator. The Creator has ordered your steps. Every single one. Stay on the right road and you will reach your destination.

Chapter 18

THE NUTS AND BOLTS - What I did - My healing toolkit.

Now, whilst I contribute my continued healing first and foremost to God/Source/Spirit/Divine Creator, I utilised a myriad of different protocols and products throughout my journey. Could I say it was 100% one or another? No. I fully believe it was a complete mix of everything in this book. I can say, however, that my research and intuition guided me to some pretty unusual natural therapies and products. Remember, whilst I was praying and believing and anchoring in faith, I was simultaneously searching for specific treatments, protocols, products and therapies to treat and heal melanoma that had metastasized in the body, especially to the brain.

There is an old saying - **God helps those who help themselves.**

Whilst God can perform immediate, overnight miracles, usually He requires that you do some work too. Whether that's outer work, or inner work, or both. Essentially it's like winning the lotto. To even be in the running to win the prize pool, you have to purchase a ticket FIRST. In other words - do something PROACTIVE to move yourself towards your goal WHILST you're waiting for things to move in a more positive direction.

I share everything in this chapter, not to say that they are a definite cure, however they one hundred percent facilitated faster healing in my body. Most are readily available for purchase from a local health food store or online and the treatments through local alternative therapy establishments or healers near you.

Consistency is the key.

Many people want a fast cure for their pain, their weight, their illnesses or sudden diagnosis, yet it's often taken YEARS of repeatedly treating their bodies like a trash can and abusing it in all kinds of ways to get to this point, so it's not going to be an overnight, one session, one supplement protocol to fix it. Obviously this doesn't apply in every scenario, more as a general viewpoint.

If you are here because there has been a diagnosis, remember all cancers are quite different - physically and metaphysically. Blood cancers and metastasized melanoma are different to tumours, along with the part or parts of the body it has been found in. Remember - everything is energy, so it's a PRIORITY to find the ROOT cause/s metaphysically and release and heal any stored or trapped emotions around that.

Take what resonates and let your intuition guide you.
Do your own research and due diligence.
You are talking about LIFE here, yours or someone close to you.
It's a BIG deal.

ORGANIC DANDELION ROOT TEA – I drank this tea, usually double bagged – probably 4-6 times every day. KINTRA brand.

"The Root chakra deals with our feelings of safety, our ability to provide for ourselves, having a stable home as well as good energy.

If you want to be more grounded and practical as well as have a strong life force energy, this tea can help you activate this energy centre which is located at the base of the spine."

This amazing little weed became my alternate to coffee and will be a staple in my pantry forever. Yes, it's a weed! BUT - this hidden yet powerful herbal tea has an abundance of health benefits!

Originally, given my extensive health background, I was well aware this little beauty would be extremely beneficial in flushing my kidneys and protecting my liver from the consistent filtering of the prescription medication. Nevertheless, my intuition served a greater purpose as I discovered the additional benefits it contained for metastatic melanoma!

Dandelion tea is rich in vitamins, is believed to be nature's richest green vegetable source of beta-carotene and is packed with iron, calcium, phosphorus, magnesium and sodium and has very powerful diuretic and liver-cleansing properties. Dandelion roots have been used in tonics and liver cures to treat skin conditions, stimulate bile production and assist in toxin removal as well as being an excellent booster to your immune system.

And whilst I knew the basics behind the health benefits of dandelion tea, once again God, my guides and intuition led me to this little treasure for another piece in my healing journey – cancer healing benefits – specifically melanoma.

The following information has been extracted from the Online Cancer Guide.

Benefits of Dandelion Tea for Cancer (onlinecancerguide.com)

Anti-Cancer Benefits of Dandelion Tea

Dandelion root extract is unique and is one of the only things found to help with chronic myelomonocytic leukaemia and it is effective in treating breast tumours. Dandelion weed is used as an alternative remedy to treat many health conditions like liver problems, lower inflammation, increase bile flow, and can treat many infections. It is also used as a laxative, improves digestion and appetite.

- Research shows that dandelion leaves, flowers, and roots hold important bioactive compounds, which have possible anti-cancer properties.
- Dandelion root extracts or tea can kill human pancreatic cancer cells without damaging the non-cancerous cells.
- Dandelion tea can kill CMML cells (chronic myelomonocytic leukaemia) has an effective alternative to conventional CMML treatment with toxic anti-cancer drugs.
- Skin cancer melanoma is known to be resistant to radiation therapy, immunotherapy and chemotherapy. The standard medical way to treat this is through surgical removal, as soon as we detect any changes in the skin but having dandelion tea can help to kill human melanoma cells without harming normal cells or non-cancer cells.
- Dandelion tea can improve the functions of the liver, gallbladder function and can stimulate appetite.
- Many clinical trials have proved that dandelion tea can help in treating cancer - related to blood, lymphoma, and leukaemia.
- Research in Canada proved that dandelion could kill melanoma and pancreatic cancer cells

"It is healthy to drink a cup of dandelion tea; you can use root, flower or leaf to make the tea. It is one of the best preventive therapies in treating cancer."

Other Health Benefits of Dandelion Tea

- The official remedy for many disorders.
- An abundant green vegetable source of beta-carotene, vitamin A, K, potassium, fibre and calcium.
- It helps to treat the liver as well as other conditions ranging from indigestion and hepatitis to depression and irritability.
- Dandelion is believed to trigger the gallbladder and liver to release bile and also stimulates the digestive system.
- Dandelion is also a kidney and bladder tonic and cleanser.

- Dandelion root contains insulin which is helpful in the treatment of diabetes.
- Dandelion greens are good in treating hormone related conditions like PMS

I was never a big coffee drinker, one a day, sometimes two in the morning if I was working away at events, so it was a great substitute in the beginning, and obviously a healthier one, to ease those initial cravings and break the habit. Whilst I had incorporated others such as Tulsi Cleanse, organic peppermint and other detox blends, dandelion became the tea of choice and remains as my one and only.

FULVIC HUMIC LIQUID – 20ml NATURAL EDGE brand
Every morning in a glass of Alka Power water
(the dose is TWICE what is normally recommended but was perfectly safe for me to do given my already existent lifestyle)

This combination probably deserves a chapter all on its own but instead I feel guided to simply share a general overview and if it calls to you then follow that guidance and do your own fact-finding and investigations.

Over the years I have found that when we allow others to go on their own journey of discovery it will often lead people to exactly where they need to be. I am just the messenger. You will instinctively know when you read what is meant for YOU.
But back to this black magic. Filled with vitamins and minerals and all of the things our bodies NEED to not only survive but thrive! Yet most of the population is deficient in true cellular nutrition which is one of the leading causes of most illnesses and diseases in the body.

Everything starts in the soil because that is where our food supply on all levels ORIGINATES from. If our soil is DEPLETED, over-farmed or heavily sprayed with chemicals then this affects the QUALITY of the soil, the level and number of minerals that our bodies NEED and subsequently the entire food chain as a flow on effect. This amazing liquid is literally reloading the body with all the minerals we are lacking.

Fulvic-Humic combined, can be attributed to interactions with ALL functions in the body; unparalleled absorption directly into cells, and vital interactions with organs and systems in the body. Fulvic and Humic are also known as lignites and have characteristics similar to shilajit (pronounced shee-la-jeet).

Fulvic does its work INSIDE the cells where it spreads throughout the system to support healthy metabolic balance, supporting proper function of vital processes. Humic works OUTSIDE the cells, in the GI tract, to encourage the body's natural removal of toxins, that in turn supports healthy immune system function. The effect is a reduction in oxidative stress to the body, strengthening cellular integrity.

Cancer also, has been linked to parasites (these can be energetic attachments and metaphysically mean certain people around you), fungus, pre-existing viruses and candida overgrowth due to poor dietary and lifestyle choices. The majority of the western population, between 70% - 85% carry parasites and candida, including children, teenagers, young adults, middle age to seniors, even our pets. My diet and lifestyle was and is, essentially clean, however I completely agree with the metaphysical meaning of parasites!

There are simple tests that can be done to determine whether you have one, some or all of these and I would highly recommend a parasite and candida detox once a year as these two on their own cause or exacerbate an unbelievable number of health issues. If you have been struggling with a certain illness or a long term auto-immune disease or feeling tired and fatigued for an extended period of time, then perhaps this is your sign to investigate hidden parasites, candida or possibly a camouflaged virus further.

Fulvic and Humic together:

- Supply essential electrical energy to revitalise normal cells
- Boost absorption and bioavailability of ALL nutrients
- Supply alkalizing minerals to encourage proper body pH
- Support the natural removal of harmful pollutants from the body
- Sustain the body's natural healthy inflammation response

A combined blend of both supplies the tools to restore, repair and nourish because of the incredible cellular rejuvenation of Fulvic, combined with the balancing properties of Humic. Depending on the purity, it can be virtually tasteless, to the other extreme of literally drinking a glass of muddy dirt. Do not be put off by any means. The benefits far outweigh a quick shot in the mornings.

ORGANIC ZINC – 1=2 TABLETS EVERY MORNING
(or organic drops/liquid)

Zinc is extremely important in immune defence. Most people are severely lacking in zinc which can cause a myriad of health issues as it is a key player in many roles in the body, including wound healing, blood clotting and thyroid function.

Zinc could also be one of cancer's worst nightmares. Researchers in a particular study, led by Zui Pan, an associate professor of nursing at UTA's College of Nursing and Health found that **zinc has the incredibly useful ability to selectively stop the growth of cancerous cells while leaving normal cells intact.** They also pointed out that many cancer patients have a zinc deficiency.

PRE/PROBIOTICS – everything starts with great gut health. I used to preach this from the mountain tops to everyone who would listen. If your gut isn't healthy then it DOES NOT matter what you're taking supplement-wise, it will be virtually rendered useless if your gut cannot assimilate and disperse it properly. Whatever you are taking, (especially in tablet form), unless your gut health is on point, then most of it will end up literally flushed down the toilet. Therefore, if you are investing in supplements, it is a given that gut health should be at the top of the list.

For anyone going through chemotherapy, the RIGHT probiotics can actually reduce the effects on the body.

"Researchers have found that improving a patient's intestinal health is a vital component in ensuring survival during chemotherapy — with some looking at **probiotics to prevent potential damage to the gut microbiota**

during chemotherapy. One such study in *Oncotarget* found that a dietary supplement with probiotics and digestive enzymes improved gut recovery following chemotherapy and antibiotics."
Extracted from Lymphoma News Today

I switch mine around usually every 6 months, different strains, different strengths to keep my gut in good health. Much like a gym routine, the body will eventually become accustomed to the same one so mixing it up can be important in maintaining good gut health. Of course, always speak to your local naturopath or pharmacy assistant, especially if you are on other medications or have key health issues or a diagnosis. Certain bacteria strains can be either targeted to your existing issue or can backfire if there are other medical issues at play. In other words, if you have no idea, don't just guess - seek professional advice.

INTERMITTENT FASTING 16:8

This was, and still is, a regular part of my monthly protocol.

Around the middle of my journey, after the brain had settled down from the radiation, I initially incorporated this for about six solid weeks, whereby I would finish my dinner at night by 7/7.30pm and then not eat again until around 1130-12pm the next day. Currently, I fast on and off depending on how my body is feeling, and of course, there are many fasting protocols.
Ones for beginners are usually 12:12 and 14:10.
Intermediate level is usually 16:8 or 18:6 or 20:4.
Professional or experienced level is from 24 hours, 48 hours or 72 hours to 4-7 days.

The 16:8 breakdown - Sixteen hours of fasting with an eight hour eating window felt good for me and my routine. I drank nothing but alkaline water and dandelion tea, and as such, didn't feel hungry at all as the tea was warming to the body and loaded with vitamins and minerals. When done correctly, intermittent fasting has an amazing effect on every part of our bodies.

Personally I didn't undertake lengthy fasting phases. Instead I simply found a daily routine that was do-able, manageable and not extreme for ME, knowing it was assisting my body to detox, weaken and starve the cancer cells of energy. This process increases macrophages, a type of white blood cell of the immune system that engulfs and digests pathogens including cancer cells, microbes, cellular debris and foreign substances. The macrophages go to work destroying these cells whilst they are in a weakened state and begin mopping up the debris in the body.

This is crucial for the immune system. It is not only giving your entire digestive system a rest from breaking down and processing food, it also gives your organs, specifically the liver and the kidneys a much needed rest too.

Fasting mimics our ancestral eating patterns and the health benefits are many, including optimising hormone levels, increased activation of stem cells, improves body composition, cholesterol and regulates sugar levels. There are a myriad of benefits, regardless of whether you or a loved one are suffering from a major illness or disease or simply looking to clean out and boost your body's natural defence system.

Of course, always speak with your health provider or a qualified naturopath or integrative doctor before proceeding. With my background I knew what I was doing, however for a beginner it is well worth speaking to a qualified integrative health coach or professional to ensure it is done correctly based on existing issues and any medications.

For those of you perhaps keen to know more, yet don't know where to begin, I would highly recommend looking up Dr Berg on YouTube for short yet highly informative video tutorials on intermittent fasting.
He is one of THE best integrative doctors I have seen as he breaks the facts down easily, keeps everything short and simple and has videos for EVERYTHING!

HIGH ALKALINE "ALKAPOWER" MINERALISED WATER – INTAKE OF 3+ LITRES EVERY DAY

Probably one of my top 3 absolute non-negotiables on my healing journey. Our bodies are anywhere between 45-75% water depending upon age, fitness levels, body fat, but suffice to say, high alkaline, MINERALISED water is essential in keeping the body and its trillions of cells hydrated and filtering toxins every single day.

Since the beginning of my journey, it was the one thing I could do and I am a firm believer that it has greatly contributed to not only improving my health overall, but also my energy levels, clearer skin and general hydration and mood. The higher the alkaline water you consume, the more hydrated your cells become, and the more water you are likely to drink. The cells and organs are now getting what they NEED to perform their functions in the body efficiently.
I will never look back.

Likewise for my tea, I continued to use my previous favourite of Pureau in my kettle, which is PH neutral. No other water has passed my lips other than these two the entire time. And of course, Chanel only drinks Alka Power while she is in my care and has rarely had more than a sniffle.

Of course, the official jury on the benefits of alkaline water is still out although for those who drink it regularly, and from my own personal experience, these are some of the health benefits you may experience:

- anti-aging properties (via liquid antioxidants that absorb more quickly into the human body)
- colon-cleansing properties
- immune system support
- hydration, skin health, and other detoxifying properties
- weight loss
- cancer resistance

"Staying hydrated is important for anyone with cancer, especially if you're receiving cancer treatments such as **chemotherapy**, **radiation therapy**, and **surgery**. These treatments' side effects include **nausea and vomiting** and **diarrhea**, all of which can cause dehydration."

I experienced NONE of these symptoms at all. Not once.

In fact, I threw the remainder of all five packets of side effects medications initially prescribed under my bathroom cupboard from day one where they have remained ever since. I never lost my appetite nor did I experience significant weight loss (outside of a few kilos when fasting extensively), there were no seizures and I never suffered from pain – other than my brain being on fire after the radiation.

I am honestly beyond grateful and blessed that by God's divine grace I was protected and shielded from these very common side effects, having witnessed firsthand what the majority do go through. It is absolutely heartbreaking on all levels and my heart goes out to anyone reading this right now whose life has been impacted in this way.

As such, cancer medications, alongside any infections you may experience, as well as your environment, can also lead to dehydration. When you're dehydrated, your body simply cannot function properly. This is because the body depends on water to perform certain functions, including transporting nutrients and oxygen, controlling heart rate and blood pressure, and regulating body temperature.

Severe dehydration can lead to low blood pressure, fever, rapid heartbeat, and disorientation or confusion. Dry mouth, fatigue, dizziness, or headaches are usually the most common indicators of a body that is dehydrated.

Bottom line - drink more ALKALISED and MINERALISED water!

CBD / THC OIL – it's no longer a dirty word - 5mcg every night

Cancer cells don't invade the body from the outside like a virus; they are created WITHIN our bodies, and they thrive by working around vitally important cellular processes like **apoptosis.**

Apoptosis is often referred to as "programmed cell death"; it is our body's way of killing off cells when they are supposed to die so that they don't become cancerous or defective.

When this control mechanism fails, cancer cells are not only allowed to survive longer and multiply, but they have the time and resources they need to develop more **harmful mutations** that enhance their ability to spread.

Of course, cancer requires many other conditions to be met to defeat the body's immune defences, but this control mechanism "glitch" is at the heart of the problem.

The endocannabinoid system and its agonists (e.g., CBD and many other cannabinoids) may counteract this glitch at the source.

There is a vast amount of information now available on CBD oil, articles, websites, and books, so I won't go into that here. I highly encourage you to research further as there are numerous benefits in taking this incredible oil regardless of what you or a loved one may be going through in this present moment.

Everything from stress management, reducing and managing anxiety and depression, better sleep, improved mood, pain management, beneficial effects treating Parkinson's, Alzheimer's and MS, lessening the effects of cancer treatments such as chemotherapy and radiation, increasing appetite and more.

My combination was prescribed by registered medicinal cannabis doctors based on the diagnosis and side effects of the medication. Every single person will be different depending on what reason it is required. I personally chose to go through an integrative pharmacy as this intuitively felt in alignment for ME.

BERBERINE 1000mg – 1 x EVERY MORNING + 1 x LATE MORNING (around 11am)

INOSITOL +IP6 – 6-8 X EVERY DAY LATE MORNING (around 11am) These cannot be taken around food so either 1 hour before eating - or 2 hours after eating and may be broken up into 3 or 4 doses (x2 at a time) throughout the day.

This is purely a summary of the fundamental basics used in my own protocol as I I have already previously mentioned the other supplements and therapies used.

MIRACLE INSPIRATION: Go with your intuition.

By all means explore, listen, question and research, however your intuition already knows the answers, and knows where to find them, if you are willing to be still and be guided.

••
"Healing yourself is connected with healing others." Yoko Ono
••

Chapter 19

WHEN THE WORLD DEALS
YOU A DIRTY HAND –
sometimes the end result may
not be rainbows and unicorns

....

"Just for the record, darling, not all positive
change feels positive in the beginning." –
S.C. Lourie

....

None of us will ever probably understand WHY certain things happen in our
lives or to other people, until months, years, even decades after the catalyst
moments, if ever at all. And it's a bitter pill to swallow when you don't receive
the answers that you feel you deserve. Especially in the moment.

This chapter is dedicated to those beautiful souls who fought the good fight,
or who have been taken unexpectedly and far too soon. Their assigned time
here on earth coming to completion, leaving many of us feeling deep loss,
shock and in many cases, totally unprepared for the volid that follows.

About 7 months into my healing, I walked into the gym to begin my usual
training session. Having been a member for many years, as in any workplace,

friendships develop, you meet new people, you interact with others and get to know familiar faces.

This particular morning, as I warmed up on the treadmill, one of the regular members whom I had formed a friendship with, approached me with a sombre expression on her face and asked had I heard the news? I looked a little perplexed.

I said, *"No? The news on what?"*
She replied, *"Remember Kayla?"*

Of course, as you may relate, there are many times in our life where you will meet people but not remember their name or remember a name but forget a face.

I replied, *"No I don't. But if you showed me a photo I most probably would?"*

She proceeded to access her phone and show me a photo, however my brain didn't register immediately and so I asked what the significance was. Her answer left me at a loss for words. *"Kayla was diagnosed a week ago with a brain tumour. She passed away yesterday."*

I was shell-shocked. I'm sure my mouth physically fell open. It was like a hit to the heart. I couldn't believe it. A week. ONE week. And she was gone. Just like that. A beautiful, young, vivacious, kind, bubbly woman in her thirties with her whole life in front of her. Gone. In just 7 short days.

I would find out as the weeks progressed that the tumour had silently grown what could only be described as octopus tentacles, spreading extensively throughout the brain, and as such had been pressing and pushing her brain to one side. Gym friends later explained that her only side effects had been occasional headaches and the odd migraine. Too far advanced for treatment and completely inoperable. She left behind a soul mate husband, a band of friends and family and those she had touched with her smiles.

It wasn't until I read a memorial tribute post the following day that I recognised and remembered her. Yes, we had sat in the infrared sauna on several occasions prior to COVID and laughed and talked about anything and all things. Work, relationships, kids, general day to day venting, fitness. I remembered she was building up her Arbonne business and always wore different shades of bright lip gloss and nail colours. And of course, always smiling. A gorgeous woman with so much life left to live. Gone.

I thought to myself, *"Why is this beautiful soul gone so soon, so fast?" Why her and not me? How can a diagnosis come back and there only be 7 days of life in between? How is this fair? Why is this happening to so many people?"*

To say it left me feeling pretty emotional and quite vulnerable that day is an understatement. It stuck in my mind and as the day progressed, I began to have serious thoughts on my own situation and wondered how she could be gone but not me? Was I just lucky? Was this her time to opt out on the earth plane? Or was I being divinely guided and protected along this path for a bigger purpose?

Backstory. Only weeks prior, in another health group I was a member in, I was tagged into a private message with two other ladies along with the beautiful woman who originally started the group. Both women's husbands had been diagnosed with brain tumours. One was about 2 years down the path on her husband's healing journey and the other was fresh out of the shock of the diagnosis. Like literally D-A-Y-S.

We were tagged because of our progress, our ability to relate, show compassion, understanding, and obviously share with her any resources or tips and direction, in her immediate days and weeks ahead. It brought up a LOT of emotion, yet afterwards, I calmly took a step back and realised just how far I had come in such a short space of time. And essentially on my own. Yes, AMAZING support around me, but at the end of the day, when the sun set and others reverted to their own work, families, homes and lives, there was no partner to talk things through with, no one to give me a strong, reassuring cuddle or hug in those solitary moments. Sometimes that is all we need to get through that very next hour, day or week. However, I was still here. Still standing. And still absolutely more than OK. I had a lot to be grateful for.

So virtually within a 4-week period, here I was, in the gym, listening to yet another shocking story, only this time, for this beautiful, young, vivacious woman, it was already over before it had even started. How does that happen?

I've said it before and I will say it again, none of us know WHEN our days are done here on this planet. None of us know when we wake up in the morning whether we will see our beds, our partners, our children, our friends, our families again THAT evening.
NOTHING is set in stone.

Every single day you are alive is an absolute gift from God and should be treated and treasured as such. Stay grateful and stay humble. No matter what the current circumstances may be. I have regularly emphasised in my conversations to others, that every man, woman and child has an invisible hourglass above their heads with virtually zero comprehension as to when the proverbial sand will run out. I shake my head in disbelief at times when I hear others, especially younger ones say they have the rest of their lives. Do you?

My brothers were tragically killed at the very young ages of 17 and 25, with their entire lives in front of them. They were fit, healthy and happy, innocently minding their own business, one out for a drive with his then beautiful fiancee and the other doing what he loved best, riding his bike with a friend. Both simply in the wrong place at the wrong time with freakish circumstances instantly taking them out. In my heart I now believe it was their time to go. God wanted them home. The sand ran out, not a grain at a time, but in one big release. Experiencing this as a young child it shattered my entire world. The grief and shock and confusion as to why, took a long time to subside. True healing only came decades later as an adult, through releasing the stored emotions and making peace within myself that they were in fact in a far better place and it was their assigned time to go.

I know of a beautiful brave mother who lost her 4-year-old daughter to a brain tumour. To put it in perspective, a person may be 26 but their hourglass is up at 28. So, in essence they are old – there are only 2 short years left on the timer. Likewise, a person may be 50 but their timer is up at 90. They are young – with 40 years of life and living left to complete. Cemeteries aren't just filled with elderly people or people who were sick or suffering from a major illness. Sadly, they are filled with beautiful, innocent little babies and children, to teenagers, young adults as well as middle aged, through to seniors. We need to stop thinking about age as young or old and think about living life NOW and enjoying each moment and each day instead.

Treasure the people, places, and things that you have around you NOW, because someone else, somewhere else is wishing they had what you currently have.

And that is usually T-I-M-E. Just one more day. In a world where followers and fame is highlighted and praised, many are so consumed with money, status and accruing material things they have forgotten the true VALUE of LIFE and the real purpose IN life.

It is one thing to live an abundant life in all its forms - we all want and deserve that - it is however, in the sharing and giving back to humanity in whatever form we can, when we can, that will lead to a PURPOSEFUL life.

A life led by SIGNIFICANCE.

Likewise, none of us really know what is happening inside our bodies at any given time. We think we do. And we could be 100% on the money. On the outside, I looked a picture of health. How many times have you heard stories of perfectly healthy people suddenly having a heart attack, or a tragic and sudden accident, or learning they have been diagnosed with a serious illness out of nowhere? It is very common, more so now than ever before and most of us know someone that fits that narrative.

Many times whilst travelling and working at company events, I would often use the analogy of the car being comparable to your body, as it is easily relatable. Every time you sit in the driver's seat and turn the key, or push the start button, you ASSUME the car will start. It's expected.

Yet, if you have ever experienced a flat battery, a failed starter motor, or any other mechanical issue that has prevented the car from starting, it is

ANYTHING but fun. It can be frustrating, inconvenient and COSTLY, especially if it is something more serious. We usually have no prior knowledge of what is going on under the hood, or any indication that something may occur because we are predominantly only looking at the car from the OUTSIDE or external viewpoint. Yesterday the car looked fine, and yesterday the car didn't have any issues. Today, the opposite.

The same applies to our bodies.

As with the car, we are usually oblivious to what is brewing internally on any given day either. The body might look and function perfectly at this moment, yet tomorrow might be a whole other story. In other words, never take your health for granted. It is one of the most important INVESTMENTS in life and has a major ripple effect on all other areas of your life if not given precedence.

Your health is WEALTH.

Typically, should the fuel light or the oil light suddenly flash on your car's dashboard, it would trigger you to find a petrol station and fill up, check the oil level or take it to a mechanic, right? If you ignore these basic signs you KNOW there will be consequences. The car will eventually run out of petrol and stop. Not what you want. Or, if you don't address the low oil, it will eventually end up destroying the motor. It can be a very big deal.

> Your body is like a car. It will get you to your destination but requires care and maintenance to run well. – Cool Bean Living

So, you thoroughly understand to not push your luck too far when it comes to your vehicle. We know they require MAINTENANCE and servicing and looking after, to continue to operate and function safely and efficiently for us. Yet when your body experiences pain or discomfort for example, and the "dashboard light" flashes, human psychology usually predicts many will "just put up with it" or reach for pain relief medication or two, or three, or have a band-aid approach to the problem.

Perhaps, as with our cars, we must begin to PRIORITISE our bodies, our health and our lifestyle.

Things can be replaced. People can't.

This hit very close to home in late April 2022 when one of our incredibly brave work colleagues, and good friend, was diagnosed with Stage 4 bowel and stomach cancer. Again, he had experienced minimal, inconsistent, and easily dismissable symptoms over an extensive period of time that were brushed off as nothing more than minor upsets. On the outside these subtle warning signs were heavily disguised and easily overlooked, yet were silently taking a stronghold internally. Within four unbelievably short months this selfless, kind, honourable and well respected man rapidly declined from looking (and feeling) perfectly fine to under-going sudden, extensive and invasive surgery, to his then heartbreaking and shocking passing on the 14th August 2022.

We had spoken often about the diagnosis, medical treatments, surgery and external protocols, always believing that he would come out the other side. Deeply anchored in his faith and trust in God, we had many conversations about departing this earth, often saying to each other (outside of Chanel) that we were both "good to go." His earthly assignment, along with his quiet, yet impactful achievements sowing seeds of compassion, humour, generosity and integrity in all he did and accomplished, was obviously complete.

Fly high Benny. Your presence in the lives of those you touched will be undeniably missed but never forgotten.

And so, coming back to these stories, we often mindlessly forget to give gratitude and grace, not only for our body, our breath and life itself - but everything – and everyone - we have in our lives. Regardless of our material status, there is ALWAYS, ALWAYS, ALWAYS something or someone to be grateful for. A reason to keep going. Something to be hopeful for. Someone who loves us and someone we love.

When was the last time you took time out of your day and truly, honestly, deeply gave thanks for the little and big things in your life? When was the last time you thought, *"I must ring/catch up with such and such"* but didn't because other less meaningful tasks popped up?

Guilty.

Many times over.

We are all human.

Work, children or other responsibilities take over.

Shit happens.

But is all of this occurring so regularly that it is now overriding that which truly matters, including others? Or worse, you begin overriding your own self-care in the quest to do more, be more and have more, ultimately suffering major burn out?

I believe one of THE most important lessons I learnt throughout this journey was to PRIORITISE not only myself and my health, but the beautiful PEOPLE who were, and are, important to me. Not the things. Not the tasks. Not the day-to-day activities that yes, usually must be done, but aren't important in the true scheme of loving, and living a purposeful, significant life.

I guarantee you will not go to your grave saying, *I wish I would've done that extra load of washing instead of simply playing for 10 more minutes with my kids*, or *I wish I would've spent more time on my laptop/in meetings/in the office than with my partner/friends/family*. A healthy balance between tasks and responsibilities and downtime with loved ones and self-care is the goal. Knowing the difference between what MUST be done and what can WAIT is the answer.

If it seems as though the scales are tipping excessively out of balance, ask yourself, what is the worst thing that can happen if I do not complete what's in front of me right now?

And, can this wait or be rescheduled?

TIME is the only thing that cannot be bought.

Like the sand in the hourglass above your head, each passing minute, hour, day, week, month and year cannot be repeated or replaced once they are gone.

Your time is the most valuable currency you have.

How are you SPENDING it?

If you are simply taking time for granted, wasting it, not appreciating it, thinking you have years or decades in front of you (and I hope you do!), eventually the day will come, as it does for all of us, when you might wish you had approached life, along with the significant people in it with a more meaningful perspective and be given another chance to repeat it over again.

> "The bad news is time flies. The good news is you're the pilot." – Michael Altshuler

When you go to bed tonight, ask yourself, *"Whose life did I touch today? Who did I help? What random acts of kindness or words of compassion or understanding did I show others? Did my friends and work colleagues hang up the phone or leave work having had a better day because of me? Did I treat myself in a way that prioritises my own health and self-care? What little things did I do or say to make my partner, kids, friends, family feel important, appreciated and loved?"*

It's a lot to think about.

Perspective.

MIRACLE INSPIRATION: Life is precious. Our time is precious. The special people around us are precious. Live every day as though it is your last. Because one day it will be. And none of us know when that day will be.

Regularly prioritise YOURSELF, your HEALTH and your TIME.

As a parent, being first priority is usually, and understandably not reality, as the world seems to influence us to be. For those with children, partners and homes this is challenging to do. It's a given that we would place our kids especially at the front of the queue.

So take the pressure off.

Perhaps a more achievable perspective is to instead HIGHLIGHT yourself and your TIME on a short list, ACKNOWLEDGING your IMPORTANCE, just not the need or urgency to be top of the list.

Instead, schedule in time for YOU somewhere in the day, the week, or the month, preferably all three, just as you would an appointment, not in an egotistical way – in a nurturing, fill-your-cup-up kinda way. Most importantly, don't put yourself last on the list in that you're essentially feeding yourself scraps.

You can't charge a phone from a flat battery bank, just as we can't be there for others until we are fully charged ourselves.

YOU time can be anything and it doesn't necessarily mean money is involved.

A cup of tea.

A massage.

A walk.

A nap.

Listening to a podcast.

Sitting down to a movie or reading a good book.

A chat and a laugh on the phone with a friend.

Getting outside in nature to reconnect.

Turning the phone off.

Or placing it on silent.

Muting or logging off social media for an hour - or maybe a day.

Waking earlier to meditate, do yoga or exercise.

Going to bed earlier so your body is rested and fully recharged.

Find whatever works for your lifestyle and whatever makes YOU feel good and re-energised, in a self-loving and healthy way.

Likewise, begin to practice this with those who are important to you.

Schedule in that phone call, that coffee, that overdue and often postponed brunch/lunch/dinner.
Check in regularly with those you care about.
Whether it's daily, weekly, fortnightly or monthly.
Leave little surprise notes in your children's lunchboxes, partner's wallet or bag.
Tell a work colleague how much you appreciate them or compliment them on their job.
Text a friend and randomly express how blessed you are to have them in your life.
Send a surprise card or flowers or a sentimental gift to your parents.

There are dozens of ways to show your love and appreciation and gratitude to those special people around you. Think outside the box. Random acts of kindness or simple messages of love and appreciation are a great place to start and usually cost nothing but five minutes of your time, yet primarily have the biggest impact.

Commit to it and watch the magic unfold as you begin to experience better relationships, better working environments, better parenting and most importantly, a better, and healthier relationship with yourself.

"Dance. Smile. Giggle. Marvel.

TRUST. HOPE. LOVE. WISH. BELIEVE.

Most of all, enjoy every moment of the journey, and appreciate where you are at this moment instead of always focusing on how far you have to go."— Mandy Hale

THE NEVER-ENDING STORY
– the end is just the beginning
- MOVING FORWARD WITH FAITH AND LOVE

> "What I've started I must finish. I've gone too far to turn back. Regardless of what may happen, I have to go forward." — Michael Ende, The Neverending Story

There have been so many little things and dozens of side stories and extensions to certain chapters that I have purposely omitted from this book. Not because they weren't important but because it would literally become the never-ending story.

I have included what I felt was important to you, the reader. What I can say is, each day is different. There are some days still, at this time, where my head feels pressure, my body feels fatigued, slight imbalances. It is what it is. I am no longer in fear of the *"what if?"*
It's become more like, *"whatever..."*

Instead, I choose to keep repeating, I AM healed and I AM all better now. The 3D body is still healing. It is still catching up. And that's ok. I love and adore and respect my body for everything it has been through and everything it continues to do for me every single day to keep me here.

My mantra and frequent response when people ask me how I am is: Every day I am grateful.
I am still here.
I am still standing.
I am still upright.
I am ALIVE!

My final MRI for the year was the 8th of December. I remember waking up that morning feeling good, feeling hopeful and feeling at peace. My rational mind was thinking, why worry. The result, whatever that may be, has already been decided. I've done my part. Just show up and do what is required.

Laying down on the machine and having the mask placed over my face once again brought up emotions and memories from the early days. As they pressed the button to slide my body inside the tunnel, I felt slightly claustrophobic. My heart rate and nerves increased but I quickly shifted my focus to healing, imagining I was instead on a Med Bed.
The appointment came and went quickly with no issues, so I simply continued on with my work commitments and usual school pick up routine. The following day was my final oncologist's appointment to discuss the scan results with Jim. I knew we would most likely have the same conversation around immunotherapy and my unwillingness to have it, yet I stayed in a place of peace and neutrality whilst I was waiting.

Sure enough, my name was called and Jim appeared to greet me. We then made small talk walking back into his consultancy room.
He said I looked well, and I acknowledged and confirmed his statement.
As I sat down, he automatically began explaining that my scans were looking great. Further reductions on virtually all the lesions that were still visible, all bar two that had remained the same. No growth detected. No activity detected. All swelling and fluid had completely disappeared. I was elated. I

had been hoping and praying for there to be NOTHING left but everything in God's timing and His way. Jim was happy. And I was beyond elated!

Then came the immunotherapy conversation and an almost immediate energy shift. He asked whether I had begun the treatments and again I said no. His face and tone once more moved from ease to annoyance.

"You know you are playing with fire Kathy."

"Yes, I do. And I appreciate your experience and valid patient concern, but everything is tracking in the right direction."

"Are you still seeing Dr Who?"
"Yes I am."

"Do you need me to refer you to a stricter oncologist?"
In my head, I immediately thought, what the hell?

Instead, I took a deep breath and politely replied, *"No, I don't thank you. He and I have a great understanding and I am happy with him."*

I could feel his irritation growing, (along with probably a good dose of disbelief), however I stood firm in my faith and conviction. Logically I understood his frustration as my response went against his experience and the familiar next steps. I'm convinced he viewed me as utterly reckless and some kind of rebel, a disruptor to the system, a maverick pushing the proverbial envelope and following my own intuitive path. And in all honesty, he would most likely be correct.

I've never been one to follow the herd. I am what many would call the proverbial black sheep. Always have been. Usually bucking the system, going up against authority, fighting for truth and justice, helping the underdog and writing my own rules. Not out of ignorance or arrogance or plain old stupidity, merely instinctively KNOWING there is another way, a better solution, a different path or simply a smarter option. Most of the lightworkers who are here at this present time have been sent in, or strategically activated NOW to help facilitate change, restructure outdated systems and help usher in new energies and higher frequencies, essentially assisting the planet in its uncomfortable awakening and divine ascension process.

Needless to say, I quickly changed the subject back to the scans and requested an explanation of the images in more detail. However in one last attempt to influence my decision and change my mind, he instead enlarged the original scans from the initial diagnosis, reiterating once more how incredibly lucky I was and that I should not be alive.

"Well, that's comforting." I thought to myself.
Then he said something that stuck in my brain.
He said **I was a miracle**, as he reiterated the severity of what I had been up against and the bleakness of the original diagnosis.

I understood from his professional point of view and experience, that he was simply doing his job, ensuring I understood the enormity of what I had faced, and was still in the process of healing from. Nevertheless, my immediate thoughts were, *"There is little hope for patients if this is the way you, or other oncologists, communicate to them."*
Imagine the mental damage to their already fragile mindset?

There are definitely other ways of conveying the same information to a person without literally destroying any positives already achieved.

My rational mind thought, *"Why can't he just say, great job. This is amazing?"*
Again, I reminded myself that this is all he knows and deals with on a daily basis. Giving people the "bad news" and automatically moving them onto the next stage in the "process".

Always remember, that someone else's opinion, regardless of their profession or experience, does NOT have to become YOUR reality.

No one rises to low expectations.

His expectations in my case, and possibly a lot of others, was LOW.

When you have a low expectation of people and outcomes, you begin to treat them in a certain way. How you talk to them. How you look at them. Right down to the time, energy and effort you put in when they are around. True?

Every day we have the capacity to change people's lives simply by the way we treat them and adopting a different approach.
Encourage people.
Inspire them.
Lift them UP.
Obviously not if they're genuine arseholes!

But imagine how different that entire appointment would have played out had he come from a positive and uplifting space?

After chatting for several minutes and explaining the nuts and bolts, he wrote another 3-month referral for my next check in. I said thankyou and wished him a wonderful Christmas and New Year and went on my way.

As I left his office, I felt good. Not only about the results, but the way I handled the tough conversations when he and the medical establishment did not agree with my personal choice. And that's ok. I was, and am, simply following my own intuition.

The hourglass over my life has simply not expired.

Remember, nothing is a surprise to God, our Creator, Source.
God SEES everything.
God HEARS everything.
God knows EXACTLY what is happening in your life.
God knows the people who are for you and the people who are against you.
God knows where you should be and where to move you away from.
God knows who should be in your life and who shouldn't.
Remember that the next time someone or something is removed from your life.
Perhaps you dodged a bullet.
Perhaps God heard conversations you didn't.
Bottom line - God knows every single person's heart and intentions.

Worrying about things isn't going to make anything better. Life is too short to be constantly worked up about something that may or may not happen. Or it has happened and there's absolutely nothing that can be done to change it. Worrying and stressing over things just depletes your joy, your energy, your time and eventually, as in my scenario, will cause your body to become run down and open to illness or disease. I cannot tell you how many thousands of hours in my life I have spent worrying and stressing about things. Some happened, some didn't, and where did all that get me?
HERE.
So moving forward - I am DONE with all of that.

God wouldn't have allowed the storms if it wasn't for our soul growth on some level. Oftentimes unfortunately, He will use the people who are closest to us - by allowing them to teach us big lessons or placing us in extremely unpleasant, heartbreaking and unexpected situations.
Sometimes, like a child, we have to experience the pain to LEARN.
Learn boundaries, learn lessons and to grow us up so we don't repeat them.

And generally when we go through pain - WE GROW THROUGH THE PAIN.
Unfortunately, it's true.
The biggest growth comes from the biggest challenges.
Nobody ever walks out on the other side of a major life event, loss or challenge the same way they walked in.
Ever.

Do what you can, then let the rest go. Give it to God. Things always work themselves out in the end. Either the situation will end, or Spirit will give you the extra strength needed to push you through to the other side.
And if the situation isn't changing, then perhaps God is isolating you and working on you to change your perspective, or your HEART, or both.

Life is too short to harbour grudges. Life is too short to hate. Life is too short to sweat the small stuff. I've been there too. Maximise what IS going right. My mother once said to me that if it's not going to matter in 3 weeks, 3 months or even 3 years, why worry about it now. Quit worrying about what can go wrong, what has gone wrong and get hopeful and excited about what can go right. Equal effort and energy output is required to believe something bad is going to happen, as it is to believe that something good and positive CAN happen.

I am still a novice, however I am committed to continuing the inner work on myself by applying this to my life daily. I am able to recognise the triggers and when and how to pull myself up.

Begin to train the default mechanism in your brain to the latter. And yes, there will most definitely be times when life events happen, and there is absolutely NOTHING you can do to stop it, although by focusing on better days, you are far more likely to emerge on the other side more at peace and better able to handle future life challenges.

I personally feel if we stop trying to play God in all scenarios and win battles that are not in alignment with our purpose, and instead, let God do what is for our highest good – then our days will be more inclined to flow, and as we master this it will eventually become a divinely-led life.
Live in a place of peace. A place of trust. It takes lots of practice and patience but it can be done.
Things may not happen the way you wanted or thought, but God's ways are better than our ways. The Divine Creator has a plan for you and knows what's best for YOU.

If you are in a storm right now, give it to God. Pray. Because endless worrying will not change a thing. Worrying is a prayer and negative manifestation in itself. The more worry you send out as a highly charged emotional energy, the more it multiplies. The way you RECEIVE a miracle is by laying the worry aside and having FAITH.
Don't worry.

Yes, do what you can do - then let the rest go.
God has it all under control.
Even when it seems everything is completely out of control.

MIRACLE INSPIRATION: Move forward with LOVE.
Love for yourself, no matter what you are currently facing.
Love for all the beautiful people around you.
Love for the little things that are going right.
You have survived 100% of your days so far.
Be proud of that!
Count the wins.
Not the losses.

Move forward in FAITH.
Faith in a Higher Power.
Faith that things will turn out for the best.
Faith that life is supporting you not punishing you, even when the skies are dark and stormy.
Faith that no matter what happens, you are being moved, directed and guided to better days.

Because you are. xxx

. . . .

> "To be grateful is to recognize the Love of God in everything He has given us - and He has given us everything. Every breath we draw is a gift of His love, every moment of existence is a grace, for it brings with it immense graces from Him.
>
> Gratitude therefore takes nothing for granted, is never unresponsive, is constantly awakening to new wonder and to praise the goodness of God. For the grateful person knows that God is good, not by hearsay but by experience. And that is what makes all the difference." — Thomas Merton

. . . .

Acknowledgments

"Every real story is a never ending story." —
Michael Ende, The Neverending Story

Throughout this life-changing journey, I have been blessed with some of THE most amazing, kind, generous, supportive souls beside me, behind me and in front of me, who took my hand and joined in with me along the way.

First and foremost, outside of my daughter, are Jay and Bianca – two of the most incredible human beings I have ever had the honour of having in my life. At the time I write this book, it has been 16 years of deep respect and love, good times, bad times and challenging times, from simple beginnings for a job interview, into a loyal working relationship, blossoming into friendship and then to an extension of family.

Those years and everything they encompassed are a book in itself! There are simply no words that could ever describe your incredible generosity, kindness, love and high level support. I just love and adore you both. This book is as much a gift to you both for your incredible belief and support as it is to those that are blessed to read it.

Thank you to my nearest and dearest friends, you all know who you are, many of my old work crew, of course my family – especially my mother who shared the same vision, same faith and same certain outcome, as well as complete strangers who were positioned in my life to drop in at the perfect divine time for a specific purpose. God has truly blessed me with some incredible partnerships, friendships and collaborations.

To each one of you I give you my deepest gratitude and appreciation but most of all, I thank God every single day, for His healing, His love, His protection and His direction and for moving me into my Divine life purpose.

A shining light in the world's darkness.
A powerful voice in the silence and confusion.
A source of strength, hope and inspiration where there may be none.
But mostly, simply being of service to others in whatever form the Creator asks of me, each and every day.
Every day when I wake up, I say GOD USE ME.

May each person who reads this book receive not only my heart-felt gratitude, appreciation and positive energy through my words, but most importantly, I pray you receive God's blessings, healing, guidance and protection over your life and His strength to see you endure and conquer life's challenges.

Amen.
Xxx

God has a tendency of choosing a nobody
To become a somebody.
In front of everybody.
Without consulting anybody.

· ·
Live your life from your heart. Share from your heart. And your story will touch and heal people's souls. Melody Beattie
· ·

236

Made in United States
North Haven, CT
21 December 2023